SELFCONQUERING

All inquiries to admin@selfconquering.com

Published by Alexander Reich for selfconquering.com

www.selfconquering.com

A QUICK NOTE

This book is not for everybody and I don't aim to please the masses or even the majority with it. Although the silent majority will be the group that agrees with me. It's just that the media will paint this differently. Anyway, with this book, I am not trying to convince anyone. Quite the contrary, I want you to make your own decisions and judgments upon what I wrote about the society we both live in.

I have been living on this planet for thirty years, and immediately I see you wondering, "what is that thirty-year-old millennial going to tell me about society?". Well, my friend. As a millennial, I am part of the loser generation, so I noticed a bunch of things, growing up in a public school, without a father, an emotionally abusive mother, no siblings, porn addiction, videogame addiction, and still managed to marry a lovely woman and thus into another great family that picked me up. I learned and observed a ton of things throughout my life, and with the quarter-life crisis hitting me extra hard, I figured I start a blog to help men overcome their own issues and to become a force to be reckoned with. While doing so, I noticed even more things getting canceled in this give up society.

I am kind of excited to see the reviews to this book if it ever makes it mainstream. Some shit like "Times change" will be thrown around, and they'll be mocking my traditional viewpoints while eating their artificial food which slowly kills their DNA. I am fine with that. Feel free to write reviews and articles that totally smack this book. I won't lose sleep over it. Which is another mindset, you, dear reader, should cultivate. People can only rustle your jimmies if you let them. If you are, in fact, emotionally hurt by someone talking shit, you actively give away power. So be reminded, I am cool with whatever you write about it. And I am totally aware that a lot of people won't like it. But if the current state of society was really that great, people wouldn't long for it to burn down in flames, would they? I will touch the apocalypse topic later on, I just came to realize that not everything from the past is bad. Like most people living healthy and with the body of Demigods by hitting the gym and not being vegetarian noticed.

So again, I urge you to make your own judgments on the upcoming pages. Maybe I am full of shit. Maybe it will open your eyes. Either way, it is sexist, alarmist, life-changing, irrelevant, triggering, obvious, helpful, destroying, fueling, pointless, retarded, and genius. At least that's what I expect will the reviews be like. Probably from the same outlet.

Let's get on a journey of what is wrong with this society where we have given up on literally anything. And how to rebel against it.

INDEX

PROLOGUE

I recently was lying on the couch and watching Grey's Anatomy with my wife. I was only half awake because I've eaten a dessert with so much fucking sugar, I could've fallen asleep before I even finished it. So I am lying there, half here, half in another realm, and I see this episode. Where there is a guy after a car accident being paraplegic. He can't even breathe without a machine. So he merely exists on that machine, can't move, can't talk, just exists. And they talk about keeping him alive. Keeping him existing in the shell of his body. Except a lot of people "live" like that today.

When did we start to drag out life as long as possible? And why? What is there to gain if you merely exist for thirty years, sobbing, and shitting your pants? The book Bronze Age Mindset covers this topic. There's much more glory in dying in your physical and mental prime. At the height of your existence on this planet, you leave it. We literally tell people they should end their careers at the climax of it. Successful football player for five years in a row? Call it quits now, before you drag yourself along, and ruin your public image until you finally overcome your own ego and quit.

Why not with life?

Why is it so much better to drag this life out as long as possible, when you literally are a burden for everyone around you, including the government? Although they probably don't care, you paid enough taxes all your life.

I guess it is because nobody really lived before that. Most people merely exist after they're about 25. Before that, when your body is young and fresh, you literally poison it with shit food, alcohol, and bad experiences. Then you get thrown into corporate life, which chips away your soul. Slowly, year after year. Every day, you sit in that moving box, alone, become indoctrinated by the radio, get into a huge box, called office building with artificial light and a ton of ruined energy from all the other people who literally hate being there. If they have a soul left, or their soul left them ages ago, and they're just human shells. You work that job, which is of utmost irrelevance to the world, humanity, and even yourself. You do it, because you have to.

And after you spend all your best years doing that, you fully give up on yourself. You are retired. No money, but also no work. So you do nothing. Literally nothing. Sitting at home, staring into another box. Why is that life?

Why did we even build that?

Back in the days, it was totally normal to train your whole life to finally die in battle at your life's prime. There was no such thing as retirement. These days, you're a paraplegic from when you're about 30. That's the average age where people give up on themselves. Physically, as well as mentally. I see a ton of people, closest friends, who literally think it is "normal" to be physically irrelevant at that age. How so? You have 30 years of retirement waiting for you buddy! You remember The Joker, right? No, the real one. Heath Ledger in The Dark Knight. No one has ever even closely resembled his amazing performance in the movie. A few months after it, he died apparently "by accident" on an overdose of medical prescriptions. No matter how he died, he died in his prime. Just laid a completely unmatched performance in the books of film and then left this world. Maybe he could've done way more great movies, maybe his career would've gone down right after that. Whatever it was. The fact he died gave the movie and his performance a big boost. People don't like to hear that, but The Dark Knight definitely was such a success because he died shortly after it. Don't get me wrong, the movie is a masterpiece, greatly written. But the death definitely gave it a push in the media. As well as Heath Ledger's performance. You just think differently about it if you know the person is dead. It's hard to put it into words, and nobody wants to say this publicly, but there is something about it that gives the last performance a certain "shine." It probably makes it more alive because the person is literally dead. And you see their last living moments. He might have literally given up on his life, we don't know for sure. But he definitely left the stage of life with a bang, instead of doing nothing. And he certainly wasn't drooling in a hospital at the age of 82.

People celebrate when they are finally out of college. "No more studying!" You spend years in college and still didn't learn the most basic principle? That you never stop learning? And most importantly, unless you want to be a mental paraplegic, you also never stop studying. The most famous Romans studied the teachings of humanity until they died. Why did we establish this society who just gives up on itself a quarter of their life in?

Some lucky guys (like me) randomly have a quarter-life crisis. Where they realize that they achieved nothing so far in their life. And then we go out and make something out of it. If you are one of these guys, congratulations, you merely avoided the accident. But you still will be playing catch-up with the guys who figured this out in their twenties. Don't be discouraged. Colonel Sanders, the founder of Kentucky Fried Chicken started at 65 years old with KFC. Sold (parts) of it for $2 million at the rusty age of 73. Doesn't matter when you start. As long as you start, and pull through with it!

We live in a give-up society. A cancel culture. We are trained from the beginning to give up. If the going gets tough, we bail. And then we blame Trump. Thanks, Trump! No, wait... that was someone else. Anyway. You read a story like that from Colonel Sanders and KFC, and immediately shit goes through your mind how you could never do it, or your mind tries to rationalize bullshit into existence, why this might not work for you.

But we weren't always like this. Otherwise we never became humans in the first place. When we got out of the ocean as small amoebas to finally discover land on earth, we didn't give up. We took some sweet 200 million years until we developed things similar to feet, so we could move our weird body out of the water. It is billions of years old DNA in us to not give up until we get what we want.

Until today. Why is today's man so different from the past?

PART 1
BOREDOM

The mind needs space to find itself and the universe. You are bombarded with notifications all day, every day. Your mind can never rest and reflect on your actions. A wise man takes time out of his day, each day, to reflect on his journey. Are you on the right path?

I add this part of the book while we are quarantined due to the Coronavirus, or COVID-19. I actually wrote this chapter before this even happened, but I didn't know that destiny, god, or green frogs will prove me right before I even release the book. I saw this lady on Twitter who tweeted that the quarantine made her realize she has no hobbies other than partying and spending money. And how it was pathetic. 400,000 likes on that tweet. And in the comments, people are saying they wish they could like it a million times to tell her how right she is. Completely oblivious to the underlying issue. And how sad that actually is. And pathetic. And I am aware that I am insulting the majority of people by saying that. But it is true, more so with women, but also a lot of men have no hobbies to speak of. Shopping is not a hobby. Other than their corporate work-life and literally slaving away all week to finally be "free" on the weekends to miss half of it because they were shitfaced drunk, they don't have anything to strive for. When the quarantine for this virus hit, two weeks in, people literally sort of died mentally. And it killed me to see this. Really, you guys have nothing else to live for? They are bored and wasting time. But it's the wrong kind of boredom. And that's where we get into the part I wrote before this virus even happened, and people weren't "forced" to be bored.

More people need to be bored. What do I mean by that? Simple. People forgot what it's like to be bored. And being bored is necessary to being creative. Finding solutions, reflecting on your actions. See where I am going with this? Modern man (and woman) jumps from notification to the next. From one job to the second, from one activity to the other. And while man is meant to take action instead of constantly talking, you do need time to reflect on what you're doing at all.

I see so many, especially younglings, just doing things to not be bored. "I am bored, let's do something." Why? Why not use that moment to watch the sun set on the horizon? Why not use that moment to reflect on the party last weekend where you got shitfaced drunk, woke up next to a dumpster, freezing cold, which ruined the whole upcoming week where you achieved nothing? Why not reflect on your mere existence in this life? Its purpose, your life's purpose? Not life in general. Why are you here? What's the point?

People are afraid to ask themselves this question, because they might unravel that their existence is pointless. Moreover, they might already, subconsciously know that, but they try to avoid asking themselves or being asked because it would show them that they do nothing of worth. I know this sounds cynical, but so is society today. It's dark, colorless, and pointless. But it doesn't have to be, when you choose to be bored. Meditating is the oldest and newest shit. Until they bastardized it again. People have devices on their head which blink when they are in the deep-state meditation. Which is a) a lie, and b) sad. Really? Can't even be bored without the need for external validation? Meditating really is just being bored. Sitting at home, doing nothing. Literally nothing. But in this nothingness, there is a whole lot of lotness. You finally get to evaluate your thoughts. Your decisions, your life. Yourself. No need to prance around that you have 1,000 Facebook friends. Nobody gives a shit anyway. Just you, with yourself. I laugh when people say they fall asleep while meditating. Really? There is nothing happening when you just chill with your eyes closed? Could be due to a bad, sugary diet. Which is also the reason why you're tired 24/7. But even then. There are no interesting thoughts popping up? A straight lie! You just don't embrace the boredom. You try to force things. Trying to force the mind-blowing next Netflix Blockbuster or bestseller book. Instead of just doing nothing.

And the reason is that you're conditioned by everyday life to be force-fed validation and communication. You don't need to communicate all the time. It is questionable anyway, if "communicating" via WhatsApp is really a proper form of communication. Emojis are not real expressions. But why is there a constant need to be informed about your friends' food? Or their newest car, leased with prison-style interest? Why do you care? I am not saying you shouldn't care about your friends, but you're not anyway. You're just depressed you don't have that car. Because you only ever see the good side. Confirmation bias. You don't know what other people do or don't do to get that life they portray on Instagram. So you give them that like with a tap of your finger, engaging their dopamine-circuit, and only making it worse for them. It is their fix. It is your fix. To feed the addiction of irrelevant likes. That like is just an algorithm turning your finger tap into a red heart symbol. The person doesn't give a shit if you really liked it. They only care about how many people liked it. Not your specific like. External validation. More likes, more of a person. You should be totally aware of this if you ever were bored! But you're not. You give out endless dopamine rushes each day, in the pursuit of gaining even more of them. If you would ever reflect on your actions, you would know. It is pointless. You gain nothing from it. Quite the contrary, it makes you feel worse.

But it is how you grew up. I did, too. External validation from Facebook, porn, videogames, whatever. Even sex itself. We're always trying to have the best sex ever, in whatever measurements you apply to this. Probably from porn. Because it gives you a sense of validation for your relationship. If your girl gladly takes loads to the face from you, she is a good girl, and you chose wisely. Can't argue with that, right? Well, really? Not even talking about her value. Talking about yours. Is that what gives you the validation for yourself? If you managed to score a girl who does all that shit? Does that make you a better person? Is that the validation you need? No. It is another form of boredom. Vanilla sex is just boring over time, right? You try to fight your biology of wanting to fertilize as many females as possible. I get it. But you're doing it the wrong way. Because you (again) try to fight it when you should embrace it. It doesn't matter at how many places you fucked, or what weird positions you tried, at some point it will be the same. Yes, because you keep trying to fight the boredom instead of embracing it. That does not mean, from now on you only go for missionary. Variety is important, but what works, works for a reason. You don't need to force variety just cause.

If you were bored with one position, you might, however, become better at it, find ways to enjoy it even more. Man does this as training. You repeat the same thing over and over until you're better at it. And when you're better at it, it is more fun. Of course, sex isn't a training field to be the best fucker there is. My point is, think about boredom differently. The mind needs space to develop. Right now, you're clusterfucked by dopamine-rushes from everywhere. Your mind has no space for new thoughts. I am writing these lines because I set myself up to be bored for an hour today. In this timeframe I planned nothing. Granted, the old Greeks, the great philosophers didn't really need to make time for such things. They just had it. Because life was very different. But man's mind didn't change. It still needs room and space to develop new thoughts, iterate on others, and come up with new ideas.

Modern society gave up on being creative. Just watch, like, really watch, modern movies. The newest trend is just making female versions of existing movies. Sure, there is some feminist movement involved in this, but the reality is, that Hollywood just can't come up with new ideas. Every Marvel movie is the same, just differently colored. Iron Man 1 and Doctor Strange, for example, are exactly the same movies in a different setting. A cocky, confident, super-rich genius guy which is also kind of an asshole gets thrown out of his life by accident or kidnapping. Needs to confront his ego, and build or develop new skills which will ultimately make him the superhero he is. Same fucking movie. Even the beard is similar. You see constant remakes of old movies, especially prone to the horror genre. I can't even recall how many versions there are of Friday the 13th. Maybe 13. If a movie becomes old enough so the current generation hasn't seen it, it will be remade with the current hype actors, some new CGI effects, and there's your $300 million box office. Recently they started reselling old videogames. It's literally the exact same videogame, it just works on the newest console or the newest Windows version, with slightly updated graphics. That'll be $50, please. Music is either an old song remade with new house-beats underneath, ruining the glory of the original. Or it is a pop song with the same beat like any other pop-song just slightly different lyrics, sung by somebody who can't actually sing, but the computer took care of that. And the root cause of all this is missing boredom. If you need to bring out a new game, or a new movie each year, and the production takes about a year, when do you really have enough time to think? When do you have time to be bored, and accidentally come up with a new, groundbreaking story? You don't. And that's why you try to reiterate people who were bored, by ruining their legacy.

ABUNDANCE

*Abundance is a false god. A wise man will
notice that true freedom is in discipline, not
giving in to abundantly available pleasures. It
also gives you the wrong perception of
everything being done, nothing to do for you,
which is a fallacy.*

Naval Ravikant said we live in the age of abundance. You literally have everything immediately without doing anything for it. I touched that topic earlier. You also know that if you do what everyone else does, you get what everyone else gets. Which is? Nothing, really. What do you get if you live the life that was designed for you? No, really, think about it. If you do what you're told, work as a drone in a pointless job your whole life. Have a wife that doesn't want any intimacy with you (anymore), and kids that become spoiled brats, because it is tyranny to discipline them. Then you retire at 70 without money, your kids hate you, and your wife probably left you for some Chad Thundercock. Well, that is pretty grim, I know. But most people live exactly in that scenario. Maybe the wife stays, but there is no intimacy at all. Do you want that? No.

In order to not get that, you need to fight pleasure. Easy pleasure is your biggest enemy. Everyone gives in to the easy pleasure; porn, videogames, sugary food, binging Netflix. Everything is there in abundance to grab. It sounds good at first, but it isn't. Because it doesn't teach you adversity. And adversity is important for you as a man. I will touch that topic later in the manly manliness section. Fighting that abundance gives you a clear advantage over your peers. Because you will actually have time. Notice how people keep saying they don't have time?

"I don't have time to hit the gym. I don't have time to search for proper food. I don't have time to pursue a side-hustle."

And then they end up spending time they seemingly don't have on 3 hours of Netflix every evening. It is not that they don't have time. It is that they rather indulge in easy pleasure instead of fixing themselves. Or pursuing something of worth. A big reason for that is obviously energy, which is due to diet, not moving, and hormones. But a cultivated mindset is another important thing. A mindset to actively avoid the easy pleasures. Growing up, you were trained into just giving in. So you will need to put in active effort to stop doing that. Won't be easy, friend. But nothing easy is ever worthwhile.

Back in the days, men had external goals, given to them by the environment. Fighting other tribes, waging war against big empires, conquering the oceans, discovering new land, whatever it was. You didn't need to search for meaning in your life, there was plenty to discover. These days, the younglings mourn the fact that there is nothing for them to do. "Too old to discover the world, too young to discover the universe." Which is just a lazy excuse. You're waiting for someone to put meaning in front of you. Why not search it yourself? There is plenty to do in this world. This is just as abundant as overly sugary food. It's just not discovering new continents, or exploring the universe, it is moving society. Whatever you want to achieve, zero-emission cars, new ways of flying, changing the intersexual dynamics, changing how people communicate, I don't care. There is plenty to do in this world. But you think everything is already done. Everything has been made already. Really? Then why aren't we deeply exploring the universe already? Why are there still people starving on earth? Why do we still burn fossil energy?

The problem is the unending abundance you see every day gives you the impression that everything has been done already. And if you give in to the abundance of pleasure, you have no drive and energy to do anything. And if you're never bored as I mentioned before, you never come up with ideas of what could actually be done. You don't need to invent ideas for the sake of it. What has worked for thousands of years, still works. This could be the other direction you go. Just like I do. Bring back traditional values because we deterred from it way too much. This is something to pursue. That can give your life meaning. It does for me. I was wasting my time with videogames and porn in the past. Now my life has meaning. I am trying to change the world for the better, with old values. Trying to raise proper kids instead of spoiled brats. Trying to keep intimacy in my marriage alive, so I don't end up like every second marriage and have it divorced. That moves me. But it is internal. There is no external drive like our ancestors had. You need to find your drive internally. This, again, is exactly the reason why people long for the apocalypse. Because a third world war or a nuclear aftermath, as bad as it might be, would bring people together (like a global pandemic?). We would have a cause to follow. Rebuilding society. It wouldn't matter what pronouns you use, or that the local barber doesn't address your transgenderism mental issues properly. You would have bigger issues at hand. And people long for this. There is a deep, ever calling scream to put your differences aside and work together to keep propelling humanity forward. I don't know where it comes from. God, nature, ultraviolet light from the sun. Whatever it is, it is deeply ingrained in any human. The need to become more than you are. More than what you were, when you were born.

That's why we have kids. They are our genetics. And we invest twenty years into one human being to make it better than ourselves. So it doesn't make the same mistakes we did. So it learns from our knowledge. For it to make the world even better than we did. That is why we reproduce. It is not just a fight for survival. It is more than that. Become more than that. Being more than you were, even after your very limited number of days on this planet are over. Your life has 29,200 days from your birth until you're 80. 29,000 isn't that much if you think about the fact that you wasted 5 days this week already with achieving nothing. Until your child is twenty years old, it lived for 7,300 days on this planet, or in your life. Make those days count. Put your knowledge into your kid, so it becomes a force in this world. Changes it for the better. Makes more out of humanity than it already was. That is the meaning in your life. But before your kid can become that, and take all your knowledge, you need to gain that knowledge yourself. You don't gain that by watching a Netflix show. The person who made that show was being creative. Changed the world by making a story into reality. You are just consuming. If you're 30 years old, which was my age when I woke up to reality and that I need to do something, then you already wasted 10,950 days of you 29,000. Sure, as a kid you don't have much control over it. But from your twenties to your thirties, you live almost 4,000 days. Did you consume in that time, or create? I solely consumed.

I hope this book found you earlier than 30. This gives you a headstart in life. What I went through is a quarter-life crisis that hits some men, but still only a minority. Some have a midlife crisis when shit is already pretty late, but even that doesn't hit everybody. Your days are numbered. But that doesn't mean all hope is lost. As I said with the KFC Sanders above. The age you start isn't really relevant. Just ask yourself right now, "do you want to exist on this planet? Or do you want to live?" The benefit of living is that you can expand the span of your life. The only way to truly cheat death is by creating something that succeeds your physical existence. Your name can survive you. The craft or art you created will succeed your body. Your life. Stop being a mindless consumer and become immortal.

CREATIVITY

*The only way to cheat death is to create
something that will outlast your decaying flesh
on this earth. Your creative thoughts aren't
limited by worldly rules. In your mind, literally
anything is possible.*

The great Achilles of the ancient greeks was the best fighter there ever was. He died in his physical and mental prime in the Trojan wars. Voluntarily almost. He kept saying these wars would be talked about in a thousand years. He knew, if he went he was going to die. A war of this size has its casualties, and despite being the best fighter ever, he would most likely die. But he went anyway. Why? Because he wanted his name to mean something. He didn't just want to be the greatest fighter in that period of time. He wanted to be one of the best fighters in history. Hence why he, and his Myrmidons actually led the landing on the beaches of Troy. He wanted to be the first one there, making his name heard and honored. He did, in fact, die in that war by an arrow through his foot, which was the mythology that this was the only place on his body where he was vulnerable. Hence why we still call that part of the foot the Achilles tendon. His name is therefore still there, thousands of years later. He cheated death. He still lives in his name. His legacy and who he was will never be forgotten. Through medicine in using his name for that tendon, as well as because he made a name for himself in those Trojan wars.

Nowadays, you don't have these kind of wars. Things changed drastically and humans are denying their own biology in which they try to fight wars at all times. By suppressing it for years, and then shooting up malls. So you can't really be like Achilles. But you can still cheat death by being creative. Elon Musk will forever be remembered as the father of the electric car. Michelangelo will forever be known for his paintings. Trump will forever be known as the funniest president. Creativity has no limits. You can apply it everywhere. It is what makes immortality possible. You can keep on living longer than your physical body through the creative crafts and arts you bring into existence. Maybe this very book I am writing right now, with nobody knowing about it, will at some time be a historical classic. Maybe I sell about five copies and nobody cares. That is the beauty of creativity. It is pure chaos. And chaos is unpredictable. But out of chaos, order can be established. And this transcendence is the root of immortality. Anything that is transformed from chaos into order will transcend time. It lives outside of established timeframes, either forever, or it comes back into time at a later stage. But it does not cling to the timeframes of physical bodies.

Now you might say that you just aren't creative, and that is where you lie to yourself. I truly believe that anyone can write a book like this. I never studied anything like that. I was actually quite bad at writing essays in school (just one more showcase how useless public schools are), my profession was in a completely different direction (information technology), and yet I am writing a book about philosophy, ancient greeks, and dying in your prime. And here you are reading it. This book from a stranger who never studied writing books or philosophy or anything like it. Do you really think you can't do it? Writing is a skill. For which you need to learn how to read first. I have read hundreds of books, that's why I am good at writing. You need to have read a ton of things before you can form thoughts you can put to paper. But the glory of it is that you learn a lot while reading. And even more, while writing. A teacher learns more by teaching his students than his students do.

Now, writing books is not for everyone. Doesn't have to be books. As I said, creativity can be applied everywhere in life. And every person can be creative. You just need to find your space in this universe where it fits. And you need to fight the abundance. If your mind is constantly bombarded and occupied with this societies abundance, you never have space to dream up new thoughts. To battle your own ideas, if they are worth it, or not. To just sit there, doing nothing, until it suddenly clicks, and you have that idea that will bring you money, success, fortune, but most importantly, meaning for your life. And thus, immortality to your name.

PART II
ANCIENT WISDOM

In our unending arrogance, we think we are currently the pinnacle of what humans are capable of. When you study our ancestors, you will quickly realize that while they didn't have the tools we have today, they outperformed us mentally as well as physically with ease.

If you are one of the lucky people who managed to make enough money so you can afford your own house. And I do mean "afford," then you probably have already realized, that this house probably won't stand in a hundred years. I recently bought a house, talked to friends who did it as well, and it was pretty apparent to me, that these days, houses aren't built to last. It needs to be cheap and should be easily replaced within the hundred years, probably less. That's how most things are built today. Brand new car from Mercedes or whatever "premium" brand you want, and it manages maybe 150,000 miles if you're lucky without bigger issues. In a museum in Germany, there is one of the old Mercedes 190 cars which managed over 1 million kilometers with the first engine. Impossible by today's standards.

This is the Parthenon on the greek Acropolis. It was build 447 BC. So it is a whopping 2,500 years old. Yes, I know the Pyramids are older, but they were obviously built by aliens. And, yes, the Parthenon is half in ruins, but after 2.5 millennia, I think that is acceptable. Our ancestors had a very different approach to life. Most things were built to last. To last very long. There is this saying, "True men plant trees in which shades they will never sit."

Just think about that for a second compared to what we do today. Nobody has that mindset. Everything is to be thrown away. The give-up society gives up on anything within a few years. Any car gets a "facelift" and an update every two years or is completely replaced. Houses last maybe fifty years with constant maintenance in between. Marriages don't last longer than 8.2 years on average. "Until death do us part." Guess, lots of people also die after eight years. Packaging for food is thrown away, instead of using reusable containers. Clothes are thrown in the trash instead of gifting them to the homeless, if they would even last that long. A T-Shirt for $5 doesn't seem to have the same lasting abilities as a really old leather jacket.

Now, if you are of decent intellect, you will realize why that is. Inflation. The companies need to make money, and due to the nature of how it is set up, they actually need to make more money each year. Unlimited growth due to inflation, because the money is worth less each year. Therefore it just doesn't make sense to build a car that lasts for 10 years, because you need more customers after one to two years. That's really all there is to it. The carmakers could make way better, and more reliable cars. They have the technology. But this actively fights their business model, so why would they do it? They need to survive. So naturally they would make electric cars, and pump them out like crazy although we don't even know if it is actually an energy plus (the energy for the cars is made in power plants, right? Which run on… fossils?), and we also don't know where to put the used up batteries, or how long they would even last.

Now, I know what you're thinking, "dude, if we never tried something new, we would still write on stone tablets!" and you are correct. We would. That is a fine line to draw. You obviously need to pioneer into new things to see what's what. But let's not fool ourselves that the rush for electrical cars is mostly driven by money. And not to save the world. Maybe except for Elon Musk, who actually started it, but 100% of the other carmakers couldn't give a damn about electrical cars until they caught on in the customer base. And suddenly, they all pump out e-cars.

The point being, that we don't need to force the "be different" narrative as we do today. This isn't solely down to electric cars. The average person is so busy trying to be different, they wouldn't even realize when they actually are different. And then what? What is gained by being different? We build cars differently than we did back then? Is that a plus? We build houses that don't last like the Parthenon? Is that good? Just because we do things differently, doesn't mean that is good. Think about it, 2,000 years later we still talk about the Parthenon because it still exists. It outlasted a ton of generations of humans. With a house build for 50 years, it doesn't even outlast one generation. Not every lame house needs to last that long, but you get my point. Our existence on this planet as humans is already limited to a very, very short blip of time. We have the ability to build things that outlast us, as I mentioned before. But we don't. Because people forgot to see why. Why did ancient civilizations build things that lasted forever?

CULTURE

The culture of a country or ethnicity is the great sum of all of its citizens and members. It is not just religion. Culture is what will outlast all of its members, and shape the future generations. And it is created by everything each of its members does and think and feel each day.

Except for your genes, the other thing you give into the life after your death is your culture. The things you teach your kids, the morals and guidelines for life you developed with your friends and community. This shapes a culture. And if it is a good culture, that makes people happy, it might survive for thousands of years. We still talk about the Romans. They birthed so many great emperors and philosophers, you can't even name them all. And not because they have unspellable names. What was one of the biggest things they did differently? They didn't give up on education after growing up. The wisest people and philosophers kept educating themselves, not for some pointless degree, but because they wanted to know all the hidden mysteries of the world and the universe. Nowadays, people think we already know everything, which displays a certain arrogance. We know absolutely fucking nothing about the universe. We may have scratched the surface a slight bit. The deeper workings are too high for our monkey brains anyway. But potentially we could understand it better, and use it to our advantage if we wouldn't give up on educating ourselves just because we graduated college. I remember when I was finished with my school education, I said to my friend what probably most young guns say at that time, "No more studying ever again!". Now I do it voluntarily in my free time.

Your culture is what defines future generations. They are

birthed in it, they grow up in it. Your environment shapes your outcome. I grew up with meeting other people outside, playing in the dirt. I was eating sand from a sandbox as a kid. Scraping your skin off because you tried a stunt with your little BMX bike? No issue, put some water over it, brush it off. The result? My immune system is utterly strong. I am never ill. I think the last time I had a cold was four years ago. This is only partly due to genes, your environment shapes your body, your mind, yourself. These days, young kids rarely go playing outside. If they meet other kids, they play on their Xbox. They don't see sunlight, and they have sanitizer everywhere. Well, what does that do? Your immune system is never tested, ergo it can't defend you for shit if you ever need it. And this is just your bodily part.

Remember in the movie 300 (which is actually historically accurate), how it is part of becoming a Spartan Warrior, that you're thrown out in the vast, cold wilderness as a kid. You need to overcome your fear, fight your way through the jungle, against vicious animals, back to the civilization. If you manage it, you come out hardened, with invaluable skills for survival. This is from a movie, but ancient civilization did that. Some indigenous tribes probably still do that or similar things to their boys. Leftists would argue this is horrifying and dangerous. Of course, it is. That's what makes it important. Danger, pain, and suffering is what makes you stronger. Shielding you from all this makes you a weakling. Our society is very feminized, so obviously, a culture run mostly by women (i.e. mothers) would never allow for such things. Because a mother rightly wants to protect her child. And that is fine and well, but a boy has to cut the bond to his mother at some point. It is important to growing up. Otherwise, you get the 35-year-old, obese virgins, playing Call of Duty in their mom's basements. And this is on the fathers! It is your job as the male parent to loosen the bond between your son and your wife. Why? If all men would forever stay with their mothers, as virgins, not achieving, our species would've long died out. It is paramount that a boy becomes a man. And a man conquers life on his own terms. He isn't bound to his mother, he does things his way. Only, and I mean that only this way, will there be enough room for another woman to enter his life and potentially bring him offspring.

This is how we humans are designed. Our ancestors knew that. Hence why we lived like that for thousands of years. Now, we try - again - to be different. Well, I am not blaming trying different things, but at this point, you have to open your eyes and see that it doesn't work. Our society has created the weakest men we have ever seen in our entire history of humanity. Not even our oldest ancestors who couldn't even walk upright were less confident, and probably physically less upright than the "men" today. A big part of it is that men never really cut that bond to their mothers, and grow up with a lot of women around. If that is your only environment, you naturally become more feminine. Because you subconsciously try to fit in the group.

All of this is part of your culture. And culture is generated by you, what you do each day, and how you act. If you are a weak loser because you grew up in that environment or culture, fine. I was like that. But it is your own fault if you stay like that forever. You can force yourself to build a proper culture for your family. That is where culture starts. In the roots of the family. If you set your family up to have strong men, feminine women, and great, educated people, then this is the culture you are actively creating. If you decide to let your kids run rampant, so they become spoiled brats, the girls fuck around, ending up worthless or feminists, and the boys become so soy, they can't even defend themselves, then this is the culture you created.

We run the baboon experiment for quite some time now. If you're not aware, baboons live in a matriarchy. The females have all the power in those societies. But if you look around, and, closely look around. Men, women, kids, society, morals, culture. It all tanked because of it. I don't see any increase anywhere. Marriages are worse which were a huge bond in families, and we know kids come out better if they have both parents. Energy is low in everyone, not just porn-addicted men. The food got way worse. Our bodies are way worse than they've ever been, man and woman alike. Kids are already obese at the age of ten. Even our pets are hopelessly overfed. Apart from the fact, we ruined a lot of species like the pug, who was once a decent dog and is now a pointless accessory for rich bitches - that dog can't even breathe anymore through our breeding - our direct environment got worse. We are exposed to artificial light all day, we can't see the stars at night. The air we breathe in cities is literally toxic. We ruined the oceans, poisoned the land, and we're even filling our nearest orbit with metal junk from old satellites.

Relationships are another big thing. Sure, back in the day, you were allowed to hit your wife with a stick that isn't thicker than your thumb. And I am not saying, ancient relationships weren't pretty tough on women. That's usually the answers I get from leftists, but as with any leftist, they are missing the point. The basis of relationships was loyalty. And that is gone for good. I recently saw a Tweet of a woman saying that cheating makes your relationship stronger. The mental gymnastics that are necessary to rationalize this are honestly pretty astonishing. And this is where even more feminists jump on me, saying that a lot of kings always cheated their wives with a ton of women. Hence all the bastard kids. Zeus is a prime example of this, isn't he? But they are wrong, again. Not to anyone's surprise. The kings did that, yes. But the kings are just the tip of the culture and society. And they sort of had different rules. For the majority of average people, cheating was not a thing. They lived together with their family and built their life every day. We're trying so hard to make polyamory a thing, completely neglecting that it will turn society into a violent shitfest. Any polygamous society tends to become very violent because most people are not happy with the state of it. The Alpha men get all the women, and the hottest women get the best men. The rest is left with nothing, which will make them bitter and resentful. Marriage was designed by men, not women. That said, these days it's mostly a benefit for women and a net negative for men. The initial thought was to bring stability to society. Initially, marriage was actually based on sex. You only got to have sex when you were married. That is what lured people in, especially the men. This way, even non-Alpha men could get some, and weren't involuntary celibates, shooting up schools. Or setting the tribe on fire. The women, on the other hand, got a provider who took care of them and protected them. Even if they didn't have the "properties" to score a high-value man. The exchange was sex. Granted, even the non-alpha men were better men than these things today, so the women probably actually wanted to have sex with their husbands, but still. Nowadays, though, women aren't really threatened in the general society. So they don't really need a physical provider and protector. Just some dude as an ATM machine. Therefore, the sex isn't really necessary either to keep him. Along with the pretty soy loser males, sex has gone down in marriage so heavily, it isn't even mentioned in the legal form these days. Back then it was a vital part of it.

So we have relationships with weak men, insufferable women, and no sex. Except for digital sex on the computer, or with other people although you should be loyal to the chosen one. Hence why people never really open up to the other person in fear of getting cucked, and therefore, all relationships stay at a shallow, surface-level stage. That easily explains why society is trying to make us polyamorous. Because if shallow sex is all you get from your relationship, monogamous marriage can't deliver that. Married sex is supposed to be way deeper, and connected. For that, you need to open up and be vulnerable. If you just need a different "type" of person every other day, porn and polygamy look daunting. But only because you don't think through what implications it will have. Or read history.

This is the culture we're giving our offspring. You won't fix the plastic-in-the-oceans-problem by yourself. But you can start by raising kids to have proper values, morals, and goals for their life, with proper, loving relationships. So maybe they will one day find a way to make the environment better for all of us. And bring culture back to something worth striving for. The old methods worked for a reason. Bring back what worked, and not what is different just cause.

THE MIND

Your mind consists of four individual parts.
All of which serve a different purpose. You need
to be aware of them if you want to gain control
over your mind and thus control over your life.

The mind is a very complex thing, isn't it? But for our everyday life, it can be easily classified in 4 states. Conscious, subconscious, the limbic system, and the higher mind. The proper term for the "higher mind" is probably something different I couldn't be bothered to research. But either way, it has been canceled pretty heavily. I make the distinction that giving in to the limbic system means giving in to your vices. Operating on the animalistic level of your existence. I.e. you have an urge to do something, and then you do it. The higher mind would resist these things. For reasons, I will get to later. And most people these days, live with their limbic system in control 99% of the time. That's why they binge Netflix for hours, watch porn when they just accidentally rubbed their dick, and stuff their face with tons of sugary, high processed junk-food.

Now, you might be asking, why would I want to resist? It's a tough mental activity when your brain literally has to fight itself. Yes, but exactly that higher mind is what discerns us from animals. This is why we are on top of the food chain. Because we learned to make use of a higher form of thinking and using cognitive ability. Physically, we have a lot of predators in the animal kingdom, lions, tigers, rhinos, you name it. They could all easily kill us. But because we learned to use our brain for more than just killing stuff, and eating, we managed to climb the food chain and take control of this planet to a certain degree (we have less control than you think, but that's another topic).

However, if we removed all our civilizational advancements,

and just put people in their current state in the jungle, we would be eradicated in no time. Except for maybe a small tribe of people who know how to hunt, and defend themselves. The rest would be food for any animal in seconds. And this unending comfort we have in our society is the reason why we stopped developing our mind. But it's not intentionally. I've been there myself. All I did was play videogames when I came home from work, while eating a bunch of sweets. The environment we live in shapes what we become. There is just no need to constantly develop your brain. You can survive with the basic functions just fine. But that's exactly what you do. Survive. You exist.

If you want to live on this planet, you need to learn. Another word for learning is discover. Go out to discover things. Physically, as well as mentally. Discover what your body is capable of, by overcoming your limbic system, and hitting the gym, learning a martial art, which is very taxing on the body and the mind. Go out and discover the depths of stoicism, discover what we know about the universe, and make your own theory on how it came about. Discover the workings of intersexual dynamics, whatever floats your boat. Just do something with this life you have. The majority of humans are really just simpletons, waiting until their life is over. When I see how people literally strive for nothing in their life, I am sad. I sort of get it, because, I mean, well, I was the same. But now that I see the light, I feel bad for these people. Maybe you are the same, and I hope I can wake you up with this book. Stop canceling your life experience! That is what you're doing if you don't challenge your mind, challenge your limbic system, and fight it each day.

Life has so much more to give than going to a job you hate, coming home to get meaningless online-achievements on your Xbox, and then falling asleep with an Insulin-spike on your couch. Think about it, for society and corporations, it is best, if you're just a cog in the system. Plugged into the Matrix, just working your job all your life, and then dying right after retirement. That's the best outcome for society. But is it the best outcome for you? Start with thinking about that, this should get the snowball rolling. Stop canceling your mind.

EUGENICS

*Humans have always sacrificed the
individual for the survival and propelling of the
collective. In fact, in history, it was a great act
of honor to sacrifice yourself for the success of
your people. But this takes a resilient mindset
not many have today.*

I'll get in trouble for this one, but let's see. Let us go back to Sparta. It was one of the most powerful city-states in the entire world. Not just ancient Greece. Sparta was most famous for its military, and especially the way it was set up politically to manage all this. But the politics aren't relevant here. They couldn't manage to create such feared and respected warriors, and virtually have the most powerful army in all of ancient history if they didn't start with it right away. It is said, right after birth, a mother would bath her newborn in wine to see if it is strong. If it survived, it was brought before the Gerousia. The Gerousia would then decide if it was killed or not. If the child looked "puny or deformed," it would be thrown into a chasm on Mount Taygetos called the Apothetae ("Deposits"). This obviously sounds harsh, but it was a first, primitive form of eugenics. If you're not aware, eugenics basically means enforcing the survival of superior genes by getting rid of the inferior people. You could say it is the way of supporting nature by its method of "survival of the fittest" with a conscious effort. Natural Selection Plus. This is said to be a Spartan thing, but we actually learned later that this was common amongst humans in general, everywhere on the globe, from simple hunter-gatherer tribes to advanced civilizations. The Spartan way in this is just pretty famous. Probably because Sparta was pretty famous in itself.

However, compare this to modern times where we canceled this completely. Eugenics in general. Actually, quite the opposite, where we try to keep any human alive as much as possible. There are many reasons for this, ranging from basic empathy for humans to the humility towards life in general. Although this is kind of hypocritical in my book since we don't care much about human life, or life in general (i.e. the state of animal farms). We put down dogs, cats, and other pets if they would suffer if we kept them alive, but a human is kept alive as long as possible, even though this is not really a life worth living. Remember the intro to the book where I talked about the paraplegic guy who merely exists? Back then, this guy would've been killed immediately. And he would've probably enjoyed it. Because there is no point in "living" such a life. Especially since you are not only not enjoying life as you should, you are a burden for society (payments for treatment), as well as a financial and emotional burden for the people around you. In that episode with the paraplegic guy, they play out two scenarios, one of which is the guy deciding to live. You then see both, him and his wife, a few years later. Both very miserable. She, because she cannot be free at all, cannot have her desires met, and have fun, because she needs to take care of him while getting nothing out of him. And he is miserable, because he is a burden for everyone around him, and he can see clearly that his wife is miserable because of him. For both, it would've been better in the long run if he died. It would've hurt short-term but would've been better long-term. So to me, this whole thing looks a lot like virtue signaling. Or mental weakness of not wanting to deal with the grief of a loved one dying.

Now, why would you want that? Well, if you are disabled in any way or not physically strong from your genes, you will fight an uphill battle your whole life. Just like ugly people always have it more difficult in life than beautiful people (I'll dedicated a whole chapter to beauty, so be ready for this later), so are disabled people at a disadvantage from the get-go. Some of them, or even a lot of them still learn to enjoy life to some degree, but I can't help myself thinking, that every time they see a normally abled person perform something they can't, they feel a deeper envy. Or sadness. Maybe they don't even notice it themselves, because you know, the mind is a master at rationalizing bullshit into existence, and they don't want to feel like victims. All well and good. But the truth and your deeper biology don't care about your feelings and rationalizations. You are, in fact, not as capable as other human beings, and thus you feel inferior.

Anyway, at this point, you will either already be steaming with hate and calling me a white supremacist, or you think I am right. But certainly, nobody is like "Meh." So let's be clear here for a second. I am aware of the drawbacks. Reducing genetic diversity, and even immunity or species resilience because you interfere with evolution. That said, this only really applies if you go all the way with this. I am not saying we look at babies and throw them in the chasm when they look weird. And I don't care about your skin color, your ethnicity, or whatever. This is creating a master race, and we know how that went. While we're at the topic. Eugenics was a common thing even in the 1900's until the Nazi regime came about. They took it (obviously) too far, and as always if something goes really bad we lean 1,000% into the other extreme and are now at a place where eugenics is a thing of the devil. And again, I am not saying we create a new master race. What I am saying is, why are we forcefully keeping clearly damaged genetic material? We don't do it with pets. We even breed them in the desired form (even though this has other drawbacks), so why not with humans? Especially if we did it for so long. So it worked, right? If destiny, God, or whoever made you have a severe disability, what use is your genetic footprint for evolution and the general survival of the species? The strongest will survive, that is how nature designed it. And if you come at me with basic human rights, I give you this: a basic human right is to roam around the world freely. But as I am currently sitting at home, and being forced not to leave my home other than if it is truly necessary due to the COVID-19 pandemic which is currently ravaging the world, I wonder where my basic human right went. This basic human right got lifted pretty quickly. Another basic human right is to not have your life taken by someone else, right? Which is also an argument of the anti-eugenics movement. Except in war times where any man who gets drafted is allowed to kill dozens of other men. All of these basic human rights and societal rules are arbitrary rules, made up by other people ruling over you. I am not saying they are bad at all, but using this as an excuse to not have eugenics is like saying we shouldn't have hygienic standards because we would interfere with evolution. We constantly interfere with evolution by keeping people alive which would've otherwise died. As well as interfering if we kill people in wars which would've have otherwise probably had offspring. But for some reason, one is more morally correct than the other.

Granted, we kind of do act on eugenics already. We can scan the unborn baby for disabilities, like down syndrome and other illnesses. And you can actually abort the baby rightfully to a certain age. At least in many countries. But after the Nazi regime went down, with it this got less and less. And since we are currently living in a pretty leftist infested society, empathy is the number one trait we have, or ought to have. So obviously eugenics are again, from the devil's workbench. Look, I know this is a tough topic, but think about all of it a bit more nuanced. The wellbeing of the individual was always sacrificed for the survival of the species. I also think people should have to pass some form of intelligence test before they are allowed to reproduce. But maybe I am going too far with this (again).

Anyway, why am I lamenting for pages about this? Well, as I said, the Spartans did this to breed the best soldiers there ever were.

It was one vital part of becoming a spartan. And the results speak for themselves. They had the strongest fighters we ever saw in ancient history. So it does work. But again, just don't do the extreme version like back then and we could have a species of purely advanced humans who explore the universe instead of masturbating to porn. Maybe?

However, there was obviously more to it. Just being born somewhat healthy doesn't make you the best warrior. The Spartans didn't stop at choosing proper looking babies. Spartan males began military training at the age of seven. By entering the agoge system. This was a rigorous form of education that focused on training the skills of stealth, hunting, fighting, loyalty, social mannerisms, some reading and writing, etc. It encouraged physical fitness and discipline. Basically, everything young men are lacking these days. Also, they were fed "just the right amount for them never to become sluggish through being too full, while also giving them a taste of what it is not to have enough." In other words, a healthy diet and fasting to develop a healthy relationship to hunger. It is also said, that young boys were expected to take a mentor. At this point, it gets a bit weird because there were apparently sexual relations involved, but as with the basic eugenics, I am not saying we need to take everything from them. That said, the agoge training, as well as basic eugenics, which I think this training is part of, would make some very great men these days. Instead of the weak simps we see each day who are "genderfluid" and complain about hairdressers not addressing them with the proper pronoun.

A rough and tough training when growing up will prepare you for the tough journey that life actually is. Obviously, it can't prepare you for anything that might be happening or not. But it certainly is a good start. What training do young men get these days? They go to public schools where they are just a number in class. They grow in body size, but never in mind. Schools were originally designed to make officers of different ranks. The plan was to have the same education for your destined rank. And if you look at how this education works, with one guy at the front, imprinting predefined knowledge into everyone in the class, it is very noticeable for what it was designed. Mentor training is much more effective because you can take care of each child's individual strengths and weaknesses. You can further the strengths, and reduce the weaknesses. Obviously, with the population exploding in the 1900's, not every child could be mentored. We just didn't have enough people. Although I need to add, the father is the first mentor a child will have. Male or female. However, with the two world wars, lots of fathers just weren't around or died. Hence why boys were raised somewhat feminized, and girls, just like their mothers, had to take on masculine roles since the father was gone. This left a big void of masculinity, which we still haven't recovered from. Other countries on earth that weren't involved in the world wars are still more "toxic masculine" today.

Anyway, I personally see a mentor training and proper physical and mental toughness training from a very young age as a form of advanced eugenics. You are not directly altering the genome - although there have been studies that a physically fit body does, in fact, change (or keep?) your genome to a certain extent - but you will create proper people which in turn create a proper culture. I will definitely train my kids from a very young age. This culture will be given into the next generation and so on, creating a better breed of humans. Thus opening up possibilities to cure diseases, explore the universe, fix the climate, and make us greater than we are today (or were). It all starts with you.

THE MENTALLY ILL

When we keep ill people alive, are we doing
them good, or are we avoiding the
responsibility of the decision out of weakness?

Let's beat that horse some more. Even if we ignore eugenics for a second, why do we have asylums for mentally ill people? This thought struck me recently when watching "IT 2" by Stephen King. Semi-good movie, but there is a scene where one of the baddies is in a mental asylum. There is this room with a bunch of mentally ill people. They sit there, drooling and shitting their pants while watching TV, or randomly exploding and performing weird actions. This had me thinking. What is the use for these people? Their loved ones aren't even around like in the paraplegic example from earlier. These people are literally sitting there with other mentally ill people, not really experiencing life (as we know), being a burden, being a bill to pay for their family, and nothing more. They cannot even express their love for the people who spend ungodly amounts of money and time on them. Imagine yourself being an alien coming to earth. Try to find a reason why we keep these people alive?

Some say they do still enjoy life (at least occasionally), or even experience happiness. Maybe, who knows, really? Fact of the matter still is, that they sit in that room or hospital and never leave it. Maybe go for a walk sometimes, but the majority of their lifetime, they will sit in that box and not see palms, huge mountains, vast desert plains, the sun set over the ocean, feel the warm wind and hot sand on an island, the cold, snowy mountains. Experience the warmth of a woman or the strength of a man, enjoy their own kids growing up, being called "mom and dad," having grandchildren, driving fast cars, building their own house, enjoying a musical or a live concert, or having a great meal in a beautiful seaside restaurant somewhere on earth.

They will sit in that box each day, doing nothing of importance. I realize I pictured a lot of you guys' lives with this. Not every one of us can experience these things. But we have at least the possibility to fix our lives, and at some point enjoy these things. The mentally ill don't. They have no choice but to merely exist in that box for years or decades until they finally die. And all of this solely because we didn't have the mental strength and grit to make the decisions which would've have been best for both parties. End their lives, so other people have at least the opportunity to enjoy it. And we comfort us with the lie that they might not know what they're missing to make ourselves feel better about the fact that we are literally torturing these people with that fucked-up life. Maybe they really don't know. But what if they do? And they know we're responsible for their shitty life?

CONFLICT

There has never been peace. It is an illusion
we tell ourselves to live comfortably. Or have
the illusion of not being threatened. War is the
nature of nature itself. War and conflict are
what propels civilizations, humans, animals,
species, and weeds out the weak ones.

The natural state of everything is conflict. Nature is fighting all the time. Animals are constantly fighting along the food chain. Fighting for survival. The Earth's atmosphere is constantly fighting the ultraviolet light from the sun. If you walk on Earth, your muscles are constantly fighting gravitation. We are constantly fighting to age. Political parties are constantly fighting each other. We fight with our spouse. We fight our urges to eat those sweets. We fight ourselves to not masturbate to porn. Tectonic plates are constantly fighting each other. Trees are fighting the wind to stay rooted. Nature is fighting itself each winter. The sperm is fighting to get to the egg. And sometimes we fight each other just for fun.

Peace is not sustainable. Because it is the exact opposite not only to our nature but to nature itself. Conflict is the natural state we live in at all times. If you really observe your everyday life, you will notice how much you are actually fighting all the time. Even if it is just your body trying to get out of bed. That is a fight. What's my point? There will never be a prolonged time of peace. Humans have fought each other for millions of years. Animals for even longer, and nature and the universe for aeons. Peace is an illusion. You think we haven't had a big war in a while in the west? Yeah, we were fighting terrorism, weren't we? And even if it isn't with guns and axes, in politics we fight all day. On the street, people fight each other constantly. We fight the inflation to survive on our minimum wage. It does not matter. You will never be at peace. We all will never be at peace. That is important to internalize, especially as a man. We all dream of that moment where we just can relax, where everything is done. We survived, we made enough money, kids are raised, wife happy, time to retire. This is what society is trying to sell you, and I'll get into detail why retirement is bullshit later. But this is a fallacy you need to overcome. You will be fighting your entire life. As soon as you accept that fact, you will finally have peace of your mind. You will still fight your urges, but you are in peace with your meaning of life. War is the meaning of life. War is life. Life is war. At all times.

So if you really want to flourish in this one life you have, you need to become comfortable with conflict. Standing up for your needs is a fight. Asking for a pay raise is a fight. Saying "No" more often is a fight. As soon as you start fighting, instead of trying to avoid it at all costs, you will be free. War is always associated with lots of deaths. But we wage wars all day. They don't necessarily need to end in nuclear bombs and millions of dead people, but accepting war as the basic state of nature will set you free. Now, I am not saying we should start waging wars just cause. There is no point in that, but avoiding conflict has become that mantra in our culture which seems off. We're not fighting back feminists and their stupid greed for power. We're not fighting back evil corporations who ruin the oceans. We're not fighting back people who put us down. We're not fighting back our own kids who become spoiled brats because we don't want to "exert power" over them. While we're fighting every day, we're not fighting enough. Because we decided it is bad. Maybe people were tired of fighting after two world wars, I get it. But there are important fights you have to fight each day. For your own good, and for the good of society. Embrace conflict as your natural state. You are human, you are nature. And so is conflict deeply ingrained in you. Don't fight it. Use it!

PART III
MORALS

There are literal rules by law. And there are meta-rules by society. The latter is built by morals. Their goal is to give order to people's behavior. A society without morals will eventually dip into chaos. Anarchy. And in anarchy, everyone tries to establish new rules. There is no order without rules.

By now you can already judge by the title of the Chapter what we gave up, don't you? Yes, morals. And this closely follows the eugenics chapter on purpose. Because this society is displaying a monumental amount of cognitive dissonance in everyday life. Leftists tell young women that aborting kids is fine. If you let yourself take raw by a stranger you just met, and you were too dumb to take care of birth control, it is fine to abort the kid because it doesn't fit your lifestyle right now. Even worse, actresses are screeching online and in interviews that aborting the kid made it possible for them to follow their career. Michelle Williams was that "woman" who said in her acceptance speech for the Golden Globe that aborting her pregnancy back then was a great decision, so she could finally win the Golden Globe. And you guys are coming at me for eugenics being immoral? Cognitive dissonance.

Now, obviously the silent majority thinks very differently about Miss Williams way of life as Hollywood does. We all know that actors live in their own bubble of self-portraying and self-praising bullshit. But the problem is, that those are the people imprinting on our kids. Parents don't do shit these days, because they don't want to break the kids' "free spirit" by enforcing rules. So the ones making rules are actors, news hosts, and pornstars. And that is pretty much what you see in the youth. Acting lives they don't have on Instagram. Sharing "news" they don't even understand, and fucking like pornstars with hundreds of partners. This is sold as "progress" when in reality it is actually backward. And very immoral.

I recently saw a Tweet where a dude pranced on Tweeter that he laid this girl after two days of dating or something. Two weeks later she cheated on him. I mean, he had it coming. Underneath this tweet was the comment I mentioned earlier of a woman saying, "cheating makes your relationship stronger." So, let's dive into the moral question here. Yes, we are at this point, where we promote cheating, polygamy, and cuckoldry because it makes a relationship stronger. It is quite the opposite. That relationship was never strong. It never existed. It was just two humans having sex. There was no relation to the other person, no love, just lust. But that's another topic for later. Humans developed morals and codes for a reason. Because it brought stability into society. We killed god, as Nietzsche said, and see what we got from it. Our current society is pretty unstable, even though it doesn't look like it. But it just needs one somewhat bigger terrorist act, and we could immediately start a new world war. And with so many nuclear weapons around, this would bring the whole world into a new dark age. The basis to preventing this are morals and codes. It doesn't matter if you take the Bible, the Quran, the Bushido code of the Samurai, or stoic rules on how to live. They all are virtually the same. Don't be a dick to people. Enjoy life, but be aware of the costs. The ten commandments of the Bible are virtually just common sense rules for stability. The first one obviously being there to enforce them. But generally, whatever rulebook you pick, it's all just:

- Don't kill people
- Don't cheat others
- Work hard, but also rest
- Honor your mentors
- Be someone others can rely on

That's virtually it. It's not that hard, is it? But these days, we do nothing. We kill people because it is convenient (abortion). We cheat others constantly. We don't work hard at all. We make fun of the elderly, parents, and wiser people than us. And absolutely fucking nobody can rely on us. Decency has been gone for ages now. In the following chapters I will outline what a decent man and a decent woman is, was, or should be. Because we neglected this for so long now, people don't even know what it's like to be someone others can rely on.

FORCED FREEDOM

We praise ourselves as the "world of the free." But rarely is the average citizen truly free in western society. Everything you own ends up owning you. A consumer society will eventually be consumed unless we create our freedom by restricting our freedom.

But why is all of this important to follow? It just limits your life, right? Yes, but discipline means freedom. See, if you give in to your vices at all times, you aren't actually free. You are a slave to your drugs, needs, and vices. Anything that makes you change your behavior enslaves you. For example, if you need to eat sugar every day, you are a slave to that addiction. You go out and buy that shit, which is unhealthy and expensive, so it alters your mode of being. Otherwise you wouldn't have done it. You probably wouldn't even have eaten something right now, but them sweets looked so nice. Therefore you are a slave to that impulse. You can't control yourself. And if you can't control yourself, you are easily controlled. Wonder why they always come up with even crazier sweets with even more sugar? Because this way they can control your behavior. You keep buying that shit, giving them money, and ruining your body in the process, feeding the pharmacy as well. If we wouldn't eat sugar at all, we would spend way less money on pharmacy and medical bills our whole life.

A different example, you go to work every day. But you don't want to, you have to. You are not free, because you need to go to work to buy the things you don't need. If you would live minimalistically, you would be bad for the economy. Now, this isn't a covert way of shitting on capitalism. I am a raging capitalist, for one specific reason. It is the only financial system that rewards people who work hard. The only way to increase the odds of truly becoming successful in capitalism is by working hard on your goals. Obviously it needs a bit of luck and timing, but it's still a better life than people being killed because they have property (communism). It is the only system that works in favor of the individual. For all other systems, like socialism and communism, you are just a number in the system. And if you have more than the other numbers, you are an oppressor. That said, capitalism obviously has its drawbacks like any system, and there are players who gamble the system. They exist in any system and society, you will never stop them. But for the majority, capitalism promotes those who work hard and add value to others! That is the great thing. You only really make money if you add value to others who buy your product. Otherwise, they buy somewhere else. And the only way to achieve all this is by having set rules for yourself, and society. If you just YOLO through your life and don't care about anything, you don't add value to anyone. You just consume, you never create. You don't live by any rules, therefore you are controlled by others. This enslaves you.

Therefore, the only way to really be free is by voluntarily not freeing yourself short-term, so you can be free long-term. This is a basic concept, nobody seems to understand these days. If you restrict yourself to the short, fleeting pleasures and money-spending habits, you will be free in the future. Money, energy, whatever. But in a throwaway society where everything solely operates in the current pleasure, I am basically talking against a wall here. So bear with me. There is this experiment with little kids called the "Kinder surprise test." You give them one Kinder surprise egg, and tell them, if they don't eat it for ten minutes, they'll get another one. If they eat it right away, they don't. This is called delayed gratification, and that is how life works. And it's a good test to see if you have some training to do with your kid. If you don't indulge in the short-term pleasure (eating the egg right away, not eating sugary food, no porn, no Netflix instead writing your book), you will have the benefits later (a second egg, a proper body and energy, proper sex-life, and success/money through your book). Obviously, in life, you don't get a set amount of time like in the kids' test. You don't know if you need to wait 1 year or 10 before you get your gratification. It mostly strikes randomly. But the basic principle is the same. If you force yourself to be disciplined now, you will have freedom in the future. Plan further than just now, plan for the future. Reap the benefits later. Think long-term, act short-term.

CONVERSATION

Deep conversation engages the mind. We dive into realms and universes the other person lays out in front of us, mixing with our own perception. Instead, we decided to listen to a monologue of dancing shadows in a box each day, where our mind is turned off completely.

Since you're reading this book, you are already different than the majority of mediocre people out there. Why? You are capable of concentrating on something for more than five minutes. People praise themselves these days with not reading books. It's "gay" or "nerdy" to read books. How in the world did that change so heavily? You are being looked down on when you read, especially complicated, books. If you read 50 Shades of Grey, that's cool, and women just do that kind of stuff, right? But reading Plato, "lol, look at this guy, thinks he's an emperor and shit."

You have to see it for what it really is. Envy. People are envious of intelligence. Which is the first sign of stupidity already. In and of itself, but also because reading books has nothing to do with cognitive ability. All you do is learn life-lessons or ways to improve/change your life. You will become a more versatile person. Maybe even learn some more exuberant words. And it does, in fact, make you a better person, because you can learn from other people's mistakes. But that is not intelligence. The definition of intelligence is your ability to learn new skills and knowledge. So intelligence is how well you pick up information in a book. This will obviously increase over time, sure. But it's not really the thing you shape the most by reading books.

Anyway, enough ranting about being called out for bettering your life, which is the default state of our current society. Books are basically long-form discussions. Most of the non-fiction books came to be because someone had a discussion about a certain topic. Either with other people or with himself. Battling an idea, going back and forth about it. Just like a podcast, right? And here is something you might notice. Podcasts are on a rise. At least among the decent people. There is the very famous, and very great Joe Rogan Podcast, and there are thousands of other Podcasts by everyone and their mother. Why? Because humans are actually capable of long-form discussions, debates, and arguing about topics. Ever since the Television was introduced, the life-span of everything went down. Not just how long a "new, exciting story" actually survives in the media, but also how long it is actually talked about in the News. I mean, watching the news is pointless propaganda anyway. But even if it weren't, you get machine-gunned with the latest news in five minutes. I remember this Australian panel where Jordan Peterson was invited, a bunch of other people up his sleeve, and the opposite, a bunch of "progressivists." Every panel member had a minute to answer a question from the audience. Think about it. A fucking minute! These were difficult, multi-layered questions. How are you supposed to answer that in a minute? The people did their best, but after a minute were constantly interrupted by the host. That was a mess to watch. Even though Peterson was on fire, and produced some funny youtube clips out of it.

The general Media and TV landscape are forced to do that because of money. As always. Screentime is expensive, so they try to cram as much stuff into their short brackets as possible. And the end result is pointless discussions, which aren't thought through to the end, which will then be force-fed to people via the News. Due to this we basically gave up on conversation. A real conversation isn't just done in five minutes. You might notice that reading this very book. I am somewhat verbose in laying out my thoughts. And I agree with Einstein who said, "If you can't explain it simply, you don't understand it well enough." But this quote has been misrepresented for ages now. I don't think he would summarize gender and intersexual dynamics in one line. Even if he cared about these things. Nuclear fusion isn't explained in one line. It's cool to have these one-liners on Tweeter, but deep philosophical topics need a bit more words and explanations to grasp the concept. And even if it just contains of examples to get the point across. We do need proper conversation!

For example, I urge you to question everything I write in this book. See it as a conversation between you and me. That's how I write my books. It is always "you" reading and me writing. I don't write for "them." This is a conversation. Yes, I am monologuing for hundreds of pages, and you don't get to answer, but sadly I can't talk to anyone of you face to face. But what you can do if you bought the paperback version, is mark pages, and then challenge my ideas via email or DM (links at the end of the book). Please go ahead. If you think I am talking shit, please contact me. I will, 100% reply. I want my ideas to be challenged. That's how conversation works. And that's how proper ideas are formed. By challenging them. Because that way you find out if they really stand the test of time. Or if you forgot something.

And if we would be talking about things more deeply, we would quickly realize how we ditched some basic morals for way too long now. The rise of extreme feminism and genderfluid people isn't just because we have too much time on our hands and no external adversity. It is also because we don't think deeply enough about things. That would happen if we would have deeper conversations. You would quickly realize that socialism might look good on paper, but if you really think it through, you will notice how it kills and killed millions of people in the past. That outcome is always the same. And there is a reason for it. But it is only revealed if you think deeply about it. The basic premise of feminism is great, but forcing it no matter what will ultimately weaken men, and in turn, weaken the family, and in turn, weaken women themselves. Because we need both genders.

So here's something for you to do. Find people you can hold long-form conversations with. I am at this point where I absolutely hate small talk. It is such a waste of my time. I can't stand it. If you don't want to engage in deeper conversations or at least challenge some basic ideas, don't bother. Maybe you feel the same. Try to find people that actually have deeper thoughts than just shallowly talking about the latest five-minute news show or the latest football match. Challenge others, challenge yourself to proper conversations. You might learn something from it. And if your friends are not that kind of people, you definitely need other friends. Don't drop all of them, I still have friends I just hang out with and relax. But I also need people I really challenge ideas with. This could also be online via DMs. Just keep your mind busy!

FAMILY

*Everything originates from the family. It is
the birthplace of a new human, and the
birthplace of culture, morals, and discipline for
the next generation. Family is what gives your
life meaning.*

I thought very long about where to put this chapter. But I think it does fit best under morals. As I already mentioned in the culture chapter, the family is where it all starts. This is the birthplace of new humans, but also of the future generations, and the values they carry. If you follow me and all the other adults on Twitter who conquer themselves, I am beating a dead horse here. But do I really? Honestly, I don't think this can be repeated enough. The traditional family is under attack. And I am not talking about tradwives and how happily they submit to their husbands. I am talking about man and woman, working in symbiont to create a proper future. Because that IS what you are doing by having children. I think a lot of people intentionally turn a blind eye to this fact. It is a lot of responsibility. If you have kids, you suddenly get handed a ton of power. Like, nuclear weapon kind of power. Imagine stopping birth control and having sex like getting the two keys to the nuclear silos. Sure, your kids are only a part of a big group of your generation having kids. But technically, your kid could become president or a serial killer. It doesn't solely depend on you, but very heavily. It doesn't even need to be president. Maybe a successful writer (wink) and influence people that way. Whatever your kids will become, you should make sure that they have some proper values and morals in place, before they go conquering the world. And they definitely don't get that by having every freedom possible. I know this sounds backward, but kids need rules to become decent humans.

So, considering how much power this yields, and how influential having kids really is, why would it be under attack? Well, if you are of decent intellect, this question answered itself, didn't it? Power. A proper family can not be torn apart, and the power they have outward into the community, society, and potentially the world can be immense. So naturally, some forces want to put an end to this, so they can keep putting their "progressive" message out. Why? Again, power. If you split the traditional family, you are left with a bunch of shallow people who don't value real connections, raise fucked up kids (like me), and who give in to their vices because there is nobody to hold them accountable. And anyone who doesn't have control over himself is easily controlled. The media doesn't just always send negative news because it sells better, it's also easier to control you that way.

Since we gave up on any sort of adversity, it's totally understandable why people wouldn't want to have kids unless they are too stupid to get their birth control in check. Kids, family, and making all of them grow is a tremendous amount of responsibility. But as I keep beating another dead horse, responsibility means power. You can literally choose what kind of values and morals you give into the new generation. So, I hope you conquered yourself first, found your own values, and most importantly, live by them before you go out imprinting them on others. Either way, having a family will shape the future way more than posting angry tweets on Tweeter. It is real-life. It does exist. And nudging a living being in the right direction is way harder than hitting "send" on your supercool outrage post.

The next chapters will be about Men and Women themselves, and what we gave up about both genders and how they should be. And one of the biggest reasons why men are weak these days, and women are insufferable cunts, is because we didn't put proper rules and adversity on them when growing up. In clean English, parents fucked it up. Everything was and is readily available, and parents couldn't be bothered to discipline their children. I am not talking with a stick, no. I hate when people come at me with their black and white philosophy. You can discipline children into proper human beings without physically hurting them. Although there is a saying that an easy slap on the back of the head does increase thinking capacity. Maybe there is something to it. At this point, purple-haired progressivists will jump on me for abusing children. Good god, I got my ass beaten as a kid when I intentionally did stupid shit (as kids do, especially boys). A bit of physical pain teaches you to behave. It doesn't make you a serial killer. But if you have no behavior teachings at home, it makes you way more perceptible to the indoctrination you will receive in school. Which is the next chapter.

SCHOOLS

If you want to know what a person is truly like, just look at the environment in which it grew up. The school is a big part of a child's life, it shapes it more than people dare to admit.

The classic teaching method we have in public schools originated from the world wars. I briefly covered this topic before. But not only does it keep your kids in predefined life paths, it also is probably the only behavior teachings your kids had. Unless you also do it at home, as you should. Now, I get it, considering how we all live in tons of debt, and both parents need to work, it is tough to discipline your kid at home. The majority of the day, it is in school. And that's where it learns the supposed truths of the world, interaction with other humans, and gets disciplined. But sadly not what you would like your kids to learn. I am sometimes astonished as to how little parents actually care what their kids learn in school. Except for history class, what kids learn in school is either heavily outdated, or leftist propaganda, rooted in pseudo-science which has nothing to do with the actual world. I know when my kids are old enough for school, I either need to homeschool them altogether, or revisit each day what they learned and set it right. Which is a ton of work, so you really gotta ask yourself why you send them to public schools. These schools teach kids not to think for themselves. It teaches them to accept everything they "learn." They are supposed to memorize stuff for tests instead of really understanding it. They are supposed to be in line with the other kids, instead of expressing their own personality in different subjects. No, behaving like a spoiled brat is not "expressing yourself." It's just bad parenting. A kid expressing itself is putting in extra hours at the schools' gym because it loves the sport, or painting at home and doing extra projects for art class because it enjoys it.

It's actually funny. In light of this I sort of like a school which has very "outdated" books and materials for the kids. Because there is at least some classic information in them, and not some "genderexpression" bullshit. The books I had in school are probably considered sexist, racist, or dangerous these days. There was this book where a kid playing with scissors and knives had his thumbs cut off. The images were the kid screaming with blood pouring out his hands. As you notice now, writing about this 25 years later, this image stuck in my head. I am aware of how dangerous knives can be. But I still use ultrasharp knives each day. Not to kill people as people would have you think. To prepare healthy food.

They also sanitize schools and kindergartens heavily, rarely go out into the forest with the kids and just play with dirt there. As always, they try to make the world more secure instead of making the kids more resilient. At 10, I was out with the school in a forest camp, building tree houses. I jumped down the house into a huge, rusty nail piercing my foot right in the middle. So what? Shit happens. I am still alive. Nothing crazy came from that. But I had a ton of fun in the camp, and it made me more resilient to pain. These days, they don't do that because it's so dangerous, and your kid might get allergies, or stung by a bee. And you wonder why these kids never grow up to become someone? Why they grow up to be weak men who are offended at being called the wrong pronoun? The school is a very big part of what your child will become one day. And unless you teach your kid a lot of stuff after school yourself, and unlearn a ton of bullshit, you are exposed to whatever narrative they're trying to ingrain. At this age, your kid doesn't understand what is right and what isn't. It eats up whatever adults put in front of it. So this is on you, my friend. You and your wife, to put your kid into adversity, teach it reality, the actual truths of the world. Make it more resilient to the tough shit that life actually is, instead of blaming others. It is on you, otherwise, you're on the peril of whatever society currently thinks is right for your kid.

PART IV
MEN

Being born a man lies a burden upon you. A burden you cannot neglect, otherwise, you will never feel fulfilled. You won't have found your place in this world. Until you do embrace your nature, you won't feel whole.

While I write these lines, I truly wonder if I accidentally exactly hit the Zeitgeist with this book. Before the global pandemic COVID-19 hit the world, men everywhere were told they are pretty much useless. Women can do it all on their own anyway, men are just horny boys controlled by their limbic system. Which is funny, because men are actually the more rational sex, but you know, if you want to push a narrative, you gotta make some shit up. However, every time some big issues like a pandemic, a catastrophe, or even a terrorist attack hits the world, the toxic masculinity to help out suddenly isn't so toxic anymore. Maybe men actually DO have their place in this world? Other than just being spam donors, and another child to take care of for the wife?

But it actually goes way deeper than this. And that will trigger a lot of feminists, and leftists, who have been pushing this "who needs men anyway?" But the world wouldn't exist as it is today without men. However, sadly, due to missing fathers (like in my case), bad role models as fathers, a feminized society telling men they are useless, and a general decline in testosterone, men literally gave up on being men. People cover this under the curtain of "progressiveness," masculinity needed to change, and all that claptrap. Really? Then see what we got from this:

- Erectile dysfunction went from <1% in 1940 to 30+% in 2010
- A 70-year-old man in 1950 had as much testosterone as a man in his 30s now
- In most marriages, the woman actually rules over the man, making him not an individual, but a slave
- Men literally have no purpose whatsoever

The last part is the key part. A purpose is what makes a man. Women's mission is to find love and connection. Man's mission is to change the world. A purpose. And as much as society tells you to level the differences, the soul remembers. That's why women are sad and unfulfilled after 20 years of "climbing the corporate ladder" and not getting a family rolling. And that's why men are sad after 20 years of playing videogames and being boozed up each weekend, instead of following a purpose. It is imprinted in our souls. Man is supposed to follow a mission. For some, this feeling is stronger, for others it is less, but if you were born with 21 chromosomes, then you need something to follow. A purpose, a mission. Getting achievements on Xbox live doesn't cut it. It has to be in the real world.

Man has always done this. Throughout history, men tried to change the world. Because they wanted their life to have meaning. We conquered land, other countries, the oceans, and even earth's atmosphere to reach for the stars, because we wanted to achieve something. To give our short existence meaning. Make our names known and heard. In the process we invented everything you ever see, we built huge civilizations, only to burn it to the ground, and then build it up again. We conquered foreign lands, we made tons of enemies, and friends with the most distant people. We conquered our own mind with philosophy, conquered time by writing books that give our teachings and knowledge to generations, thousands of years apart.

But in recent decades, man has given up on his inner fire. It is still there, but buried underneath fleeting pleasure like porn, pizza, and pounding women. If you even manage to get a woman to put out. And even if you do lay a lot of women, filling a lot of voids doesn't fill the void in your soul. Great men don't bother themselves with constantly having sex. They have bigger things on their mind. If you are like I was five years ago, you will now probably rationalize some reasons into existence. "I just have a high sex-drive," "I love sex, so why drop it?" "It's a great bonding mechanism, man!" and all this stuff. Those were my thoughts. Reasons as to why hunting for the pussy is occupying most of my life. Until I found my purpose, and now this has way more pull on me than any woman. And I am in my physical and mental prime, loaded with testosterone, so trust me, that is not the reason. But I found my inner fire again. The drive to change the world. Which is why I am sitting here on a Sunday morning, writing these lines, instead of playing PUBG like I used to do. I was hunting for a sense of accomplishment. A sense of achievement. But winning an online game really does nothing. You might climb an artificial ladder and have your anonymous name move up the ranks of other people. But what do you really gain from that? This game will be gone in a few years, and if you were the number one of its ladder really doesn't matter.

However, writing these lines and waking people up to what they are missing in life might change some of you. For the better I hope. I can't control people, but I can try to help them understand life better. This is what men are supposed to do. Mentor other men. If you have kids, then this comes naturally. You raise your kids and try to make them decent people. At least you should do that. Unless you are like my father who couldn't be bothered. Although I have to admit, that this is a lesson on its own. So he wasn't fully useless. But it doesn't need to be kids, you can mentor a lot of people just like that. Or other kids. Become a trainer for a fighting school, so young boys learn to enjoy adversity. Also, I always urge everyone to write a book. Every person has a story to tell, especially as you get older. You naturally encounter shit. That is life. It throws curveballs at any given moment. And generally, you learn from it. And what did you learn? I don't know, because you don't tell anybody! You think your life isn't special, but that's wrong. Any life is unique. We all have different shit happening to us at different stages in life. Write it down. You don't even need to sell it, just put it on one of the free outlets online, or a blog, or whatever. But teach people, that is one of your many purposes.

ADVERSITY

Since conflict is natural and the basis of
everything, and adversity inherits conflict, you
need to seek that on your own. In this current
society, adversity is not present inherently. But
you will never grow yourself, if you never fight
for anything.

We live in a society where we don't face any issues at all. I've talked about this before, no real struggles, no real problems. You think you have real problems? Your ancestors would laugh at you. You know where the word "Marathon" really comes from? The Persians landed at Marathon in Greece, so Pheidippides, a Greek man was sent to Sparta to ask for help. He ran 240km (150 mi) in two days and back. Then he ran 40km (25mi) to the battle near Marathon and back to announce the Greek victory over the Persians. Before he died. Probably of exhaustion. You, my friend, can't even run up two flights of stairs before you almost die. That was a different kind of man back then.

Now, obviously we don't need this kind of man today, because we have all sorts of comfortable transport methods to get us there, sitting, stuffing sugary food in our mouth to be even less able to do something like that. But my point is, you don't even know what your body is capable of. But you would know, and most importantly, you would enjoy it, if you would put yourself into adversity.

Adversity is what makes a man. We aren't made to sit in front of an eye-damaging screen all day, ruining our posture. We are meant to move! Heavy movement! This requires you to overcome adversity. To put yourself into pain and struggle. But why would you do that? You don't need it? Yes, because we gave up on it. A muscular body is still the beauty ideal for any man. Other men want to look like you if you're jacked, and women want to be with you and want you in them. This hasn't changed. Dad-bods are not a thing, my friend. Your wife might tell you, she likes a dad-bod, but what she really says is, "A small belly is fine, but you should have a huge upper body to compensate for it." But even if we don't care about what the woman likes, trust me, building your body will change your relationship with your flesh vehicle. Once you improve yourself, and make something of yourself, you will increase your confidence. Because you know this is what it should be like. If you have a belly right now, or you are skinny fat, you know this isn't right every time you look into the mirror. You might rationalize it due to your job or whatever bullshit reason you come up with, but the fact of the matter is, that you are neglecting yourself. Because you restrain from adversity.

The physical is just the easiest display of it. If I see someone who is obese or fat, I know immediately what kind of mindset they have. And this has me never proven wrong, once. They always end up blaming the government for not having money, the industry for making bad food or they not having time to hit the gym. These people are lazy, and therefore their opinion is invalid. Triggered? I hope so. Maybe you will wake up to your own bullshit. You will hate me for saying this, but you know very well you hate yourself for looking like that. And notice how this isn't about how others perceive you, although this is a big part of it, it is how YOU go through this life. Your body radiates who you are. If you are too lazy to get that in order or don't have enough grit to put down the sugar, then everyone, including you, knows very well you act like this everywhere else in life. And this is why you don't achieve, and why your soul hates you.

Everything that is gained easily, is worthless. Because everyone can do it. And if it becomes easy, it loses value. Because adversity is what makes it valuable. You have to overcome yourself, or other obstacles to achieve it. THAT is what gives it its value. For example, a woman that is easily laid, isn't really that good most of the time, right? Doesn't feel so crazy. But if you finally get a girl to put out after some kind of resistance, you conquered her. That adds a feeling of accomplishment to it. The same with porn vs. sex. You literally had to overcome nothing to get to sex. Which was evolutionary tough to come by. Only 1 in 17 men reproduced back in the days. And you didn't have sex daily. So your body is programmed to give you a sense of accomplishment every time you have sex. If you actually manage to get to have sex with a woman, then you accomplished something. Especially if she isn't of the easy type. If you fapped to porn, you accomplished nothing. That's why you have that deep feeling of nothingness in you afterward.

The masculine grows with challenge. But challenge is hard to come by in the current world. So you actively need to seek challenges. Whatever you like doing, try to be the best at it. The masculine soul is competitive by nature. We want to fight other men (not women), we want to be better than them, stand upon them after we fought them to the ground. That is why participation medals are truly retarded. You were here, here's is your prize. What? I didn't do shit! I remember when I received such a medal as a kid (obviously from a female teacher), and at first it felt nice to get that medal. But then I saw that every kid gets it, and that kind of ruined it for me. Because it wasn't special. It actually made me feel worse, because it visually showed me that I am not special. This medal was useless, it was an insult! I just didn't realize it back then. If you get the winner's medal, the first prize, that is a different feeling! You ARE the best, at least for now. All your effort in becoming that person, all the adversity you had to go through finally paid off. That is the feeling your masculine soul is seeking. But it is hidden behind fear, adversity, pain, struggle, anger, drawbacks, and wanting to give up. That's what makes it valuable. Not everyone can and will achieve it. Only a few selected who overcome all that and themselves to go after it, against all odds. And if there is a winner, there must be a loser, virtually by definition. This is why these participation medals exist. So nobody loses. But this also means nobody wins. You need losers to have a winner. And leftists try to remove "losing" out of society because it feels bad. Of course! That's the point! It shall make you feel bad, so you go out and get better! Fix your issues, train harder, so you don't have that negative feeling again! So if you get a participation medal, throw it into the face of the person giving it. Because it is an insult. They are literally saying you can't achieve better, and are trying to pamper your feelings. They are telling you that you are weak, and you should be angry about it. So angry, that you fight hard to be the best. To get a proper medal. To be a winner.

ENERGY

*The masculine energy can be an immense
force of will, life, and glory. Your presence
alone can change the mood and outcome of a
situation. Learn to cultivate and preserve your
energy, unravel the strength in your mere
existence.*

In the current political climate, men growing up hear the term "toxic masculinity" all the time. Mostly from toxic women, but anyway. Be ready for this: That term is very broad, right? It could mean literally anything, and that is how it's used. To paint everything as toxic they don't like about men. But anything that is put so broadly is also wrong. Broad strokes cover a lot but miss details. So, men, let me say this, your masculinity is not toxic by definition. Be aware that society, in other words, the Media, is actively trying to put you down. But what is there to gain? Well, weak men that work their jobs without question, and never stand up for something make good worker drones. Yes, the Media is really just an extended arm of the corporate world. And the corporate world needs you to spend the majority of your healthy life span to work and not ask questions. Remember the movie The Matrix? From 1999? Probably not. You should watch it, in this movie The Matrix is the world you live in. "You pay your taxes, you go to work, and you help your landlady carry out her garbage" is a quote from the movie. But The Matrix is just a computer program, designed to keep your mind trapped in it, so they can use your body as energy. In the movie it is a machine world, basically an artificial intelligence, using the thermodynamic powers of the human body to produce energy for their needs. And they created The Matrix to keep you going to your work. That is what society wants you to do.

They only need your energy, to work for their company so they can enjoy life. They show you all these fancy things, sports cars, huge mansions, vacations to the Bahamas. But can you ever afford that? If you work really hard, does anybody really notice? Maybe your supervisor, and you might get a promotion. Then what? You have a new supervisor and the whole thing starts anew. Yes, some can climb the ladder so highly they actually make decent money. Working 80 hours a week. Congratulations. Feels like slavery? Because it is. There is more to life than working for someone else.

If you were to leave work tomorrow, just not show up. Would anybody notice? Your supervisor, right. But the big heads of the company? The people running it? Would the world come to a halt if you just didn't show up? Now, YOUR world would stop, because you'd be fired. But the world itself wouldn't care. Not a slight bit. Because you are just a cog in the system, nothing more, nothing less. It's funny, for the longest time I thought I like being that. I literally said it, "I like being a small cog, helping the company run." That's how deep the conditioning was ingrained in me. Now, I can't even remotely connect with the person I was back then. Sure, not everyone can become Elon Musk and change the world at large, but I know very well, some of you clearly seek for something bigger. For meaning in their life. It doesn't even have to be something big like becoming a best-selling author, or head of a company, or curing cancer. You can make the world better day by day. By teaching kids, yes I come back to this. You can do it on the sidelines. I still work a 9-5, because writing books hasn't set me free (yet). But in my free time, I feed the need in my soul by writing these lines. You have a similar passion in you. That is your masculine energy. And this energy is so utterly powerful, you can't even believe it. You have it every time you watch porn. What? Yes. Notice when you actually try to restrain it. If you're horny, dick hard, and you try not to watch porn this time, not to rub one out. It is insanely tough to not do it.

And this isn't because you are just a horny boy, operated by your limbic system. It is because your inner fire needs some form of accomplishment each day. And porn is the easiest for now. But imagine what you could achieve if you learn to channel that energy into something else? Imagine if you would do pushups until you're exhausted every time you want to rub one out. You have so much energy at that moment, that would make you buff in weeks. Imagine you learn to channel this energy into something creative. Or into building something. That is also how I tell men to overcome their porn addiction. Divert the attention somewhere else. And every time they do it, they discover how much power they actually possess. How much that burning flame in them can propel them to achieve greatness. To lift the world! You don't know it yet, because every time your soul calls, you give in to the easy pleasures, for that false sense of accomplishment. But once you learn to channel it into something more meaningful, you will be surprised how much power being a man actually yields.

PHYSICALITY

"No man has the right to be an amateur in the matter of physical training. It is a shame for a man to grow old without seeing the beauty and strength of which his body is capable." –
Socrates

I talked a lot of shit so far. But how to actually get it going? Well, the first thing you MUST have set in place is your physicality. There is ZERO margin for chill with this. This is the basis for everything. Whatever you want, success, women, sex, better intellect, better friends, better image, confidence, more self-love, adversity, even spirituality, everything starts with your body. It is the flesh vehicle for your consciousness and your unconsciousness. It is your temple. And you have been shitting over that temple for decades. It is a sacred vessel, which has been ravaged with unholy actions. It is time, you bring this thing back to shine like the sun.

Why is it important though? Your body is the physical display of your mind. Lazy body = lazy mind. There are zero exceptions to this. Because your mind operates IN this body. If the body can't operate properly, how is the mind supposed to do this? Imagine your body like a car factory. How reliable and well-working the car coming out of the factory is, depends entirely on what kind of materials you put in in the first place. If you have weak metal (sugar), deadwood (no movement), and thin plastic (bad sleep), the car at the end (your mind) won't be working properly. Or break apart real quick.

People give me a lot of shit when I judge their mind by their visual appearance. You know, "beauty from the inside" and all that claptrap. Yes, you can be a good person while being fat, sure. But I would neither want to work with you (lazy), and neither want to reproduce with you (bad health), or be around you (bad environmental influence). See, I am not telling anyone to do anything. I am just saying, I DO judge you by your appearance, and that is my right to do so, plus if YOU want to change something about your life, if you want to achieve, and win, then this is where you must start. And again, this isn't just for visual appearance. This does a lot for your own mind, how you portray yourself, what you think of yourself, and how you see the challenges of life. Successful people all are generally pretty fit. Actors, businessmen, entrepreneurs, whatever. They are all thin (with some exceptions proving the rule). Why? Because they know they perform better mentally, if their body performs better physically. It is a symbiont. You cannot divide the two. You just can't. Back in the days, roman emperors and philosophers were jacked as shit. Sure, they had to do a lot more physical labor than we do these days, but that wasn't the only reason. They knew that the body is the basis on which all things form. Hence why they kept their body running properly. Humans naturally knew this until we developed all kinds of technology and artificial food to literally numb us. Rome was one of the greatest empires to ever see the world's surface. It stood and fell with their men, great men, great, jacked men. You don't need the physique of Achilles, but you absolutely need to develop a basic human physique that doesn't hinder your everyday movement.

The majority of people literally give up on their bodies at the end of their twenties. After years of machine-gunning it with alcohol, maybe drugs, absolutely trash food and fucked-up sleep schedules, they kind of forget about caring for it. I remember how I, myself, talked about this. "I am thirty now, life is over!" I said this making fun of the fact that I was totally unfit with friends who were similarly unfit. Why do we live in a society where this is the norm? Usually this is said in the same breath as "sex going down in marriage is just normal." Do what everyone else does, and get what everyone else gets. I decided not to have that shitty life, giving up on everything in my thirties. So I decided to make conscious effort to preserve my flesh vehicle as well as I can. The first thing was an inspection. Where have I been neglecting it?

So I changed my diet completely. Reduced carbs as much as possible throughout the day. Reduced sugar to a minimum, and even did a 30-day no sugar challenge, and still do that occasionally. I got myself a proper gym routine and started working out properly. Not just moving around a bunch of weights, I LIFTED. HEAVY. Finally put some load on my muscles, got myself some proper protein sources, and saw my muscles grow in weeks. This is where you absolutely must start. If you are obese, you need to cut sugar and carbs immediately. And you need to MOVE. You don't need to run a marathon. Be realistic. If you are physically fucked up, you need to start slowly. Re-read the chapter "THE MIND" to set your mind right for this. Changing your diet, especially if you ate a lot of sugar, takes a strong mind. Sugar is an addiction for many people. Yes, it is a drug. You will notice it once you drop it for longer than a week. Every time I completely drop it, I get crazy headaches after about 3-4 days. This is normal, because you have withdrawal symptoms. They only last for about a day, so don't worry. But if you experienced this once, you will realize how bad this stuff really is. Our ancestors didn't eat sugar at all. We know this diet is bad for the human body. It drops your testosterone levels by 25% for about two hours, it makes you insulin resistant, thus reducing your possibility to grow muscles, and, well, it makes you fat. So here's something to give up on: sugar. Try it yourself, and see your body flourish.

After you've fixed your diet for a few weeks, you will notice how much ancestral superpower you suddenly have each day. If you also move your body every day and get 8-9 hours of sleep, you are a new man. Trust me, if you keep doing this, you will never want to go back. We tend to go from one extreme into the other because we never want to fall back into old bad habits. So you might end up becoming a sick bodybuilder, or an Adonis-type athlete. But what's so bad about this? I noticed a funny thing. I truly started to enjoy the male physique. I know people will call me gay for this, but once you build and develop your body, you really learn to enjoy the greatness of man. What you are capable of, and how powerful your body can look like. No, that doesn't mean I masturbate to naked men now. But loving your own body not just by the power it inherits, but also how it looks in the mirror, as well as other men's effort to looking good is a great mindset. I told you most roman philosophers were jacked. They truly enjoyed the physique of man as well. We all already enjoy the female body. It is great. But the male body is great as well. If it is built properly. So build it, and learn to enjoy both human versions of the body.

LEADERSHIP

*When you came into being in this world, by
winning the race to the female egg, you were
leading that race. You won, because you were
first, and the strongest. Throughout a man's life
the need to lead will never end.*

Any man will have to lead at some point, even if you don't lead yourself all your life. If you want to have kids and family, you need to lead. You will be the captain of your family. And you would actually want to do that, because it has great benefits. Women like a capable, leading man, so she will gift you with her gifts if you lead the family properly. If you don't lead, then she will take that role, unwillingly, because it is a man's job to lead. Our basic biology makes us leaders, but men have been neglecting this role for decades now. Probably due to the responsibility it brings, and because most men are so weak these days, they are afraid of their wives shitstorm if they screw something up. Which, is utterly weak in and of itself. You'll learn why in the upcoming chapters about women. But what you are neglecting is immense power. This always baffles me. Everyone always longs for power in their life. They want people to behave their way. Want to be president because they would do it so much better. But the tools for power any person has at hand are never used.

Leadership means power. You get to decide what you want to do. What your family is doing, how your life is going to unfold. Why would you not want that? And you DO have that power, you're just not aware of it. Or you are afraid of wielding it. There is this saying, "Do not fear power, fear those who wield it." Unlimited power can be a path to the dark side, and this is the basic view society has these days on power. Anyone who has power is automatically a tyrant.

Any powerful person is obviously part of the Illuminati, secretly plotting the destruction of the world, so lizard Nazis can reign again. Even if you just wear a suit, and you're a billionaire, you obviously made a pact with the devil to gain that power. But it's all just projection. Because these people lead themselves, and thus gained the power any person has within them. And if that power is evil or not, depends 100% of who you are. Because there is a difference between leading from strength and leading from tyranny.

This image mocks your boss, but you get my point. A tyrant has slaves. A leader has followers. You can only lead from strength if you managed to lead yourself first. This is the basis to lead a family properly. You need to have overcome yourself, and know how to lead your inner feelings, thoughts, behavior. If you sit at home, being the tyrant, your family might listen and do what you want. But it is out of fear, not because they want to. This can even be a thing in the bedroom. While dominance is a great factor in bed if your wife puts out because she has to instead of doing it because she wants to then you're a shitty leader. Judge a man by how his subordinates talk about him. If your kids and wife talk greatly about how you have your life in order, then you are leading well. If they don't talk good about you, but still do what you want, you're on the path of the tyrant. This is true for any place. Work, friends, etc.

A great leader is someone who doesn't care about people following him while still caring about them. This sounds paradoxical, I know. Look, Twitter is a great example of this. You cannot force people to follow you on Twitter. There is no way to do that. They need to click the button. So if they click it, they follow because they want to. They want to follow your lead on things. But you still care for what they say, you engage with them, you try to aim your products at your target audience. You give them what they want, but you don't force them to buy it. This only works if you are fine with yourself. If you need the external validation, it doesn't work, because you are hellbent on them following you, and you get mad if they don't. You can achieve this mental resilience if you are fine with who you are. No matter what other people say. And for this to work, you need to lead yourself. You need to be able to stop yourself from falling victim to all your vices. Once you overcome most or all of your issues, you are at peace with yourself. You have control (as far as it isn't an illusion, you know?) over your life. And because of this, you will radiate a certain calmness. And this calmness, confidence, and "know what you're doing" will attract people. Women and kids more than anything, but also other men. The best Admirals and Sergeants are the ones that radiate calmness in tough situations. The soldiers need guidance, mental strength, and clearance in their leader. They put their life into their leader's hands. And so does your wife and do your kids. Their life is what you make of it. For this, it is vital that you have conquered yourself before you have kids.

Now, you might be frightened by this. If you think about it how you are literally responsible for how the lives of wife and kids turn out, this is a lot of responsibility. Isn't that a pretty weak thought? Why are you frightened? You're just frightened because you don't believe in yourself. You think you can't do it. But why? Because you've been a fuck-up all your life? Well, then why don't you go out and get your shit together? Rather binge Netflix? See, this is why I said a leader needs to conquer himself first. Overcoming your own vices and issues gives a certain self-worth which can't be bought. It can only be earned. You cannot even fake it. Only when you truly know who and what you are, because you overcome adversity, only then will you subconsciously radiate the calmness that attracts people. And, people being attracted to you has all kinds of benefits, don't you think? So here's your plan. Overcome your issues and vices, gain that crucial self-confidence, which will automatically reduce your fear, and then make the life of everyone around you better, which in turn, will make your life much much better. Show society what a great leader is and that power doesn't mean tyranny.

BROTHERHOOD

If you want to know what a man is like,
look at the environment he surrounds himself
with. If you want to revel in your deep
masculine energy, you need to put yourself in
the masculine energy of your brothers.

Too many men these days spend too much time with women. And too many women also spend too much time with men. To revel in the depths of your gender, you need to be around more people of yours. It is what creates your energy. We naturally adapt and absorb the people we spend most of our time with. As the saying goes, "you're the product of the five closest people around you." If you're a man, and you spend the majority of your time around women, or even your woman, you naturally tend to pick up feminine energy and radiate it yourself. As well as your woman will pick up your masculine energy, and become more of that.

In ancient Sparta, the men were not permitted to live with women, even their wives, until they were 30. They grew up solely with masculine energy, which prepared them for life. As well as women were only in a group of other women. If you have been in a relationship, you remember how hot and awesome it was in the beginning. When you couldn't see each other every day, you had dates, they were full of desire, lust, and love. The sooner you live together, the sooner this "new thing glory" leaves. If you see each other each day, there is nothing special about the occasion of seeing that person. You do it anyway. Routine comes in. The thrill and excitement of finally seeing the person again after days of abstinence is awesome! This struck me quite heavily after I moved in with my girlfriend back then. I thought we'd be fucking like mad, finally living together, no parents who could accidentally walk in.

Little did I know that this also took away a big part of the thrill and excitement.

Imagine living in ancient Sparta. You were married at 25-ish, but you couldn't live with your wife. Every time you meet her it would be new and exciting. Every encounter would be full of desire. You wouldn't want to sit on your phone while the person is next to you. You would want to know more, touch more, feel more, be more!

However, these days, society tries unbelievably hard to make everyone equal. Which means boring. The polarity between the sexes is what makes it interesting. The more this polarity is leveled, the more boring it becomes. There are no differences left, nothing happens when both meet. As a soon-to-be father, I realize there are times, where you need both together at all times. With a baby for example. While in the first few months, you can't do much as a father, you definitely need to be around for your kids. Yes. But here is an important part. If you really want your marriage to survive and work out, you will need to incorporate alone time away from your spouse. And this is where the brotherhood comes in.

For some reason, we tell men that true brotherly love with your friends is "gay." We tell them, being around men too much makes you unfit for a woman. Because the only goal for a man in life is to have a woman, right? See, at some point in your journey of waking up, you will realize that the woman in your life is a nice addition, but really not much more. Your bros are where you really shine. Your friends are the ones that tell you what you are doing wrong, how you are fucking up, and what you should be doing. Your brotherhood is fundamental to your health. Being around other men, absorbing their masculine energy, and giving out yours is what you need to be closer to yours. Remember, you need the polarity between the sexes to fully embrace the possibilities. The stronger the polarity is, the more intense the tension between the poles will be when you finally meet. The more you both revel in your genders' nature, the stronger the sex, lust, love, and relationship will be. To recharge your polarization, you need to meet with men. Hang out with your buddies. And your woman needs to be around other women who do the same regularly. If you ensure this, your relationship will be great.

Which is why it was actually a bad idea to mix sexes in all possible everyday life situations. For example the gym. Mixed gyms aren't good in my opinion. I have been to gyms for 13 years now, and whenever guys are exercising and a woman in her tight yoga pants comes in, they fuck up their workouts. And it's not because she is such a stunner, it's because suddenly there is competition. The female energy creates a void in the masculine flow of things in the gym. Guys try to outperform the other guys, because of competition to impress the woman, for the off-chance of something happening. Between men, there is obviously competition as well. But it's easier for a man to take a loss over the other guy if it's just for that competition than to take a loss over the woman. This has been amplified by a society who tells you that the only goal in your life is to marry a great woman, but it's also part of nature of displaying your great genes to reproduce. Remember, this is our limbic system's number one goal. So, whenever a woman is around, men behave very differently.

For this, I think we need men's only gyms, men's only bars, sports places, etc, etc. Just going out only with buddies isn't gonna cut it, when one of you is constantly checking out the hotties at the bar. We need male-only spaces so men aren't competing over a possible (or impossible) chance of the female wandering by being impressed. But to improve themselves, improve their masculine energy. If you hang out with friends, and there is a woman in the group, this is a whole different energy than when you were just the guys. Everyone notices that, but nobody thinks deeper about the implications. You hold back, you don't say what you really think. You maybe even try to impress her. You cannot be truly who you are. Around men, you can. Sure, there is competition as well, but you're not trying to get into anyone's pants. You are open and free with your expression. True as you are. You need this for your mental sanity. And for this, you need your brotherhood. If you don't have many male friends, you absolutely need to go find them. Make new friends, which is also a great training for social skills. But especially, if you are in a relationship, you need that masculine environment to replenish your manly energy. And the time away from your girl will not only increase the tension between both your sexes, but it will also make you miss the other person. And make meeting again, exciting. As it should be.

THE WARRIOR MONK

*The best man is the man who could bring
down an entire civilization but decides not to do
that. He has the skills and power to change
everything. But he also lives in the wisdom of
being aware of that power.*

If you truly want to achieve peace within your life, this is the title you need to develop in your mind about yourself. This will need years of training, physically, as well as mentally. But it will truly set you free. You don't specifically need to know how to fight to be successful. But combat will teach you a lot about humans and life. At some point, if you are successful, and you are making a lot of money, you will realize that money isn't that important. It is a store of energy. And it's not even a good goal. If anything, you want to be wealthy, not rich. Rich means, having a certain amount of money or networth. Wealthy means, you get a certain amount of money periodically transferred to you. Rich can be gone at any second. Wealth is built upon assets that don't die out quickly, so they keep giving you money. Doesn't even need to be much. Especially not as a monk.

Once you are at that stage, and you wonder if there is more to life than just fast cars, lots of women, and big mansions, you will be searching for peace. Inner peace. And that is achieved by being able to kill people but not doing it. Confused? You might be familiar with the quote from the Bible:

Blessed are the meek;

For they shall inherit the Earth.

Sadly, this has been widely misunderstood for ages. Probably a bad translation. The World Bible even translated the "meek" as "gentle" which is worse. Jordan Peterson among other famous writers said, that this was misunderstood. The Greek word "praus" was used to define a horse trained for battle. Back then, they brought wild stallions from the mountains and broke them for riding. They used them to pull wagons, race them, and the best ones were used for war. They kept their fierce spirit, courage, and power, but were disciplined to respond to the slightest nudge of the rider's leg. They were the best and most reliable horses around. They could charge into battle at thirty-five miles per hour and come to a dead stop with one word. They weren't frightened by arrows, spears, or torches. If a horse had these traits, it was said to be meeked.

These horses embodied power under control, they were submissive to their masters, but certainly not spineless. This is what meek really means. And suddenly it paints a completely different picture about that quote from the Bible. The meek shall inherit the Earth. Let's put it in clean words. The strong, but disciplined, trained in combat, but try to avoid it, fearless but not dumb. These people shall inherit the earth. And that is what the warrior monk archetype is. The warrior is trained in all kinds of battle. He knows how to defend himself, and he has the skills to kill one or many men with the blink of an eye. But he is disciplined not to abuse this power. He doesn't just go out and kill people. That would be a tyranny and not a nice place to live. For example, most men are physically stronger than women. But a real man doesn't use his physical dominance to make a point clear. That is tyranny, and the wife will always live in fear. He uses his strength to protect his family from external forces. So the wife happily submits to him on her own. Not by force. That's the difference between a great King, where people happily follow him and work for him, and a tyrannical King, who reigns by force and with slavery. Both get the work done, but only one protects you from getting backstabbed by your citizens.

The Monk part comes in when you're not falling prey to your vices. Go into monk mode for a week. No phone, no TV, no computer. Go out in the wilderness with a tent, and a bit of food. Even reduce the food to a minimum. Enjoy fasting, and see your mind go to places you've never been before. You will also notice you don't actually need any of these things. You are fine with yourself. Your body, your mind, your soul. That is all you need. Some - especially Japanese - fighting arts will teach you these things as well. Read about the Musashi and the Bushido. Great books about the Samurai Era, which arguable was home to the greatest warrior monks there ever were. These men were trained in the arts of taking or giving life like no one else, while also restraining from all vices. This is about as good as man can become. And if you reach that stage, nature allows you to rule over Earth. And since you are nature, this is finally the time where you will rule over your soul. Not by force, by design. You become one with yourself. So go out, restrain from the bad eating habits that ruin your body. Restrain from porn, video games, and meaningless sex. Learn a martial art, learn how to fight, how to protect. Develop skills to make sure of your own and your family's survival. Learn how much power is inherited by doing so. But also learn how to not abuse your powers. You will learn how to do this by slowly getting more in tune with yourself. By not caring about others' approval. By being fine with your own, and on your own. And then, you will finally be an honorable man. It is a long way to go. But it is a worthy path. Not everyone can be the warrior monk. It takes a lifelong dedication to be that man you were designed to be by nature.

PART V
WOMEN

The feminine is your direct opposite. She works in completely different ways. If you want to revel in her and enjoy the tension of both opposites, you need to know how the feminine operates. Through this process, man will learn a lot about his own nature. Because both sexes need each other.

I am going to reference the Bronze Age Mindset (again) right here and now. He said women, are actually closer to animals. In a good way, relax you screeching harpies no one wants to touch. Animals live fully in the present. At all times. They don't care about the past or the future. Because both states do not exist, and, well, they don't have mortgages to think about and how to pay them off in three decades.

Women are similar. I always said, women constantly live in the now. It doesn't matter how great of a man you've been to her in the last 20 years if you fuck up today, you've always been a fuck-up. You might think this is stupid, and I can't blame you. I thought so for the longest time. But I wouldn't call it stupid now. It has its benefits. Because if you've been a loser throughout the whole marriage, you can literally turn it around in months if you fix yourself, and she'll suck your brains out. You're just too focused on the negatives, aren't you?

But is the manly version so much better? Men do think in the past and in the future. If my buddy is being a royal asshole recently, I still like him, because I remember the ten years of great support from him. He's been a great guy, so being an ass in the last two weeks is just a phase I guess. Or is it? Maybe he changed for worse? That would suck! See where I am going with this? Man is prone to overthinking!

I guess that is why the Christian God is always portrayed as an old man. An old, worrying man. The male was created in the image of God, and thus he inherited his power. Sure, we can't create planets. But we do create life. I know women prance themselves with creating life when they're pregnant. But technically, they don't. The sperm is already a living being when it leaves your dick. The egg is stationary. The sperm needs to move to the egg. Obviously, it needs to have some sort of consciousness to do that. The woman nurtures the life you created. By no means is her part less worthy, but creating life is a man's job. Hence why it's so important you stop splurging your literal life-force into napkins by watching other people have sex via pixels on your screen. Sperm is created from the most potent blood cells in your body. Every time you ejaculate, you steal a ton of energy from your body. Use it wisely.

Anyway, back to the point. I always imagine god as a worrying old man. Did his creation really work out? Did he make a mistake? Is there something wrong with the world? Should he come in and fix it or not? So many thoughts! This is the problem of man today. Overthinking. It is said that a man acts instead of talking about it. Well, that was probably the case back then, when man didn't invent so much shit which constantly keeps his thoughts occupied.

Think about hunter-gatherer times. If you were out hunting, waiting for your prey to come along, you had a ton of time. Sure, you might've been starving, but we know for a fact that fasting is actually healthy and boosts your thoughts. So these men were out, thinking about stuff. But they weren't overthinking. Because there wasn't so much to think about. They had the hunt, the family, the tribe, rarely sex, but it happened, and war. No mortgages, kindergarten, left-wing teachers, transgender, gluten, soy-latte from Starbucks, oil-changes for your car, expiring credit cards, fifteen different insurances, and that fucking hole in your brand new v-neck t-shirt. None of this was a thing. And thus he had time to think. About real things. Why he is on this planet? What his tribe is doing? Is he raising a proper child? Stuff like that.

You might be wondering why this chapter is called "whamen"? Well, you need to see the difference. Because the general population keeps saying that women are constantly overthinking. But it's wrong. Women are overfeeling. This is also known as the Hamster. Just like the spinning wheel, a hamster jumps in, so her thoughts are spinning like crazy sometimes. When you say something without exactly disclosing how you feel or what you do, you engage her Hamster. This isn't rational in any way of the imagination. It is purely, and 100% driven by feelings. And the more she hamsters, the deeper she gets herself into that spiral out of which she will be certain that you cheat on her. Man always thought this to be weird (again) but it's wrong. It is useful if you know how to use it. Because, if you engage her hamster she actually thinks about you. A lot.

The best women live a lot in their feelings. You might be thinking this means a ton of nagging and tantrums. Of course, but it also means blistering orgasms, a bubbly, happy woman doing tons of shit for you out of pure joy and love. You are, again, thinking too negative. Women are told that this is bad. Serving a husband makes her weak. Well, women are the weaker sex. You can try to fight it, but it won't achieve anything. It is for both sexes best, if they accept their nature and embrace it. Well, it would be easiest to just not listen to society, that would make your nature come out on its own. Because in true fashion of a cancel culture, it will tell you to give up your nature. Your nature of a rational male. Your nature of a feeling woman. Both sexes are designed as a symbiont. Man alone is way too rational and constantly thinking about all kinds of shit. A woman's feelings teach him there is more to life than just seeing. The woman alone is way too emotional and making bad decisions. A man's rational and guidance will bring her the greatness of actual life. And when both sexes come closer together than physically possible, in penetration, as well as in their souls, new life is born.

A woman is at her best when she is not aware as to why she does certain things. I don't mean romping strangers she just met and is confused as to why she took that dick. I mean when she loves a man, but she doesn't really understand why. He is kind of a jerk sometimes, but also such a good man. And a great lover, giving, but sometimes selfish. The variation keeps her happy, and her own ignorance as to why that is.

SUCCUBI

*The archetype of the succubus has many
men brought to the brink of existence. A wise
man is aware of the cues of this hellish type of
woman.*

You might be familiar with this image of the female, either from some Dungeons and Dragons videogame or from porn. Either way, the succubus is a female demon, which uses the power of her female "assets" to lure in men and suck out their soul. This can be taken quite literally, yes. The succubus therefore plays right into the weakness of a weak man who can't resist a woman's sexy body. Hence why these characters are usually quite revealing and slutty. And while this made for a great collection of porn videos, these do exist in real-life, except that they don't look exactly like that. But there are a lot of women out there who literally suck out your soul if you keep being around them. Remember, women feed off of attention, and if she is constantly in need of pampering of her feelings, constantly needs your attention, and flips her shit if you don't respond immediately to texts, she is a succubus in disguise. Or as they call themselves, "High maintenance."

You would want to avoid such a woman as much as possible. I understand why she can lure you in. Not just with the sexy looks, but probably also because she is fire in bed. Does everything you want and all that. I get it. But staying with her you give up on your life. She will drag you down into hell where she originated from. That won't be pleasant. Some call them energy vampires, so you might be familiar with that term, but I personally like the succubus version more, because it implies the sexy part, which is a key thing of such women to drag you into their fangs.

A proper woman has her own life, and No, "shopping" is not a hobby. You would be wise to search for someone more unconventional as a life partner. Unless all you care for is meaningless sex, which, in itself is meaningless and therefore pointless, you should search for a woman who has her own life. Not only is the occasional distance between you two important, but it also means she doesn't need to feed off of your attention constantly. Like literally all the time. If your current girl has nothing to do all day but scrolling Facebook, and buying shit she rarely wears or uses, then you found yourself a succubus. Or one in the making. She will suck your life-force out. Either literally or metaphorically, and you will give up on all your aspirations as a man. Sooner or later. You will give up all your hobbies, your friends, maybe even family. And while some of the people around you might actually be bad for you, and your girl would be right to have them removed, ultimately it should be your decision. And if she is on her knees right or soon after such a talk, you know you're being tricked.

Now, obviously not all women do this intentionally. If they grow up without a strong father figure and sex being at full display in the media 24/7, she has a hard time grasping how she can be of value for a man other than on all fours. Most women end up pretty damaged because of this. They usually have sex early, and it's all they know. They are pretty annoying outside of the bedroom, because you literally can't do anything else with them. They tend to be pretty masculine in the behavior (not visually), because they never had a strong masculine figure to polarize against, and, well, because society tells them it's great to be a strong woman. Y'all need no man, right? These girls then tend to end up in relationships all the time, because the men they are with give them something to live for. They adopt what the man is getting from life by adopting his hobbies and even friends, or they just want to be around him all the time to feed off of his life and the glory of it. They cannot fathom to build it themselves, or even be themselves and enjoy it. The clinical term for this is codependent. If you have a girl that literally can't be at home for a day without getting bored (not the good kind of bored I mentioned earlier, literally flipping her shit because she doesn't know what to do), you have a codependent woman. This does happen in men, more so these days, but I think this is mostly a female occurrence.

Here are more signs to vet your girl, or any future girl, for codependency:

- They focus on other people and their problems most of the time
- They're extremely self-critical, but never show it
- They feel responsible for everyone and everything
- They are perfectionists
- They experience high levels of guilt and shame
- Intimacy, open communication, and trust are difficult

Considering how self-secure a succubus is always portrayed, you might now be wondering how this plays together. Also the intimacy part, because all they want is sex, right? Well, it's all a show. The succubi try to fill the deep void within them. I am aware of the mental image, yes. Since they constantly focus on others and their issues, they never address their own problems. They might even suppress them. And try to fill the subconscious realization of having no personality with sucking of personality traits from others. You will quickly realize that a succubus of that kind will adopt the way you speak. She will get angry over the things you get angry, etc. You will blind yourself with thinking you found your soulmate, but in reality, you just found someone who mirrors you. And while the woman, as I said, is just a mirror of how well you developed your personality, she should still be her own person. That is the important distinction which makes this whole thing difficult to describe.

Intimacy might be happening a lot with her, and even crazy stuff, because she is trying to please you as much as possible so that she can keep sucking off of your life. Even if a woman has severe body image issues (usually unfounded) she will do crazy shit. Like public sex, or hot lingerie. However, she doesn't really do it because she likes it (which an experienced eye will notice) but because she tries to please you. She will probably feel a ton of guilt afterward, as well as she would feel a ton of guilt if she doesn't please you. Here's a simple example: If you can't get it up, a healthy woman will either comfort you or call you out as a weakling, because as a man, it is on you to perform (and because you fap to too much porn you womble), the codependent woman will blame herself for not being sexy enough. This will really shatter her self-esteem because now she can't even give you that thing (she thinks the only thing) that keeps you with her. So if she talks shit, you got a healthy woman. If she is sad, it might be questionable. If you feel bad, you're a weak cunt, and you need to stop fapping to hentai midget porn.

Now that you know what kind of women these succubi are, you need to be aware, that you usually attract such a woman into your life by total accident, or, more likely, because you're fucked-up yourself. I am a firm believer, that like attracts like. This can even be observed with most long-term couples. The exceptions obviously prove the rule. So if I described your current girl above, chances are, that you have some issues yourself you would need to address. That said, reality is that most people, or most of these women, may have some codependent tendencies in them. They can still end up being healthy individuals, even if they show SOME signs of it. The codependency then usually comes out full force if such a person is with another somewhat broken person. For example, you've been a beta loser male all your life, you're passive-aggressive, and backbiting, and you come across such a girl. Recipe for disaster.

None of you will be really healthy, and you will push each other's illnesses.

If you managed to address your issues, afterward you're either so pissed by your current girl that you ditch her, or you take on the hard task of helping her overcome the codependency (which is possible but takes a lot of facing tough childhood feelings on her part). That is up to you do decide. And please, my friend. Don't look at any girl like she is a succubus from now on. Guys are way too quick on putting labels on women. And especially if it takes away your responsibility towards yourself, this is an easy call. I wrote a whole book about why you need to own your shit (that is its title). Always think of the positive when meeting new people. Since you are here in this book, you NEED to read the chapter on positive femininity later. Otherwise, your outlook on women will be pretty grim.

FEMININE ENVIRONMENT

The feminine is like a flower. Put her in
good soil, and she will bloom into the most
magnificent, beautiful, breathtaking form
nature can produce. Put her in bad soil, and she
will suck out the energy from everyone around,
and be a source of despair.

Before you are too afraid of any woman that shows cleavage from now on, let me teach you an important fact about women. Women are almost 90% malleable in their behavior. I told you about the mirror before. That she mirrors your personality in a way, that if you are more masculine, she will become more feminine. This isn't made-up at all. There are hundreds of success stories out there of men who changed themselves (even decades into a sexless marriage), and their wives came around fully. Feminine, sexy, wet hot in bed. Now, why is that? It is mostly because the feminine is a follower. They like following a strong masculine force, so they can keep their attention coming. The succubus, as I explained before, is the dark version of it. But the light version will make your life much better. The feminine is capable of making everything better or worse. The feminine is an amplifier. You give her sperm, she turns it into a real human. You give her a house, she turns it into a home. You give her guidance, she turns it into a win. You give her attention, she turns it into a fun experience. You give her love, she turns it into more love, warmth, and beauty. And, well, if you give her dick, she turns it into fun.

But all of this heavily depends on the environment you create as a man. She can also turn your kid into a spoiled brat. She can turn your attention into a fight. She can turn your home into hell. And you giving her love can be turned into nothing but resentment and hate. The feminine fully is what you make of it. How she grows depends on what soil you put her in. Let's have a practical example. We all want our woman to have long, beautiful hair because it is feminine and sexy. But such hair is a lot of maintenance. If she has to worry about money because you fucked up the finances, and you don't get your ass up, she would want to reduce the things to worry about, so the hair gets cut. Less stress, more focus on other things. You want her to wear nice sundresses and cute lingerie in bed. But do you even have the money to buy these things? And do you create an environment for her where she feels safe in her body to wear such skimpy outfits, or does she feel judged every time she puts on nothing but a tiny string?

That's why you see a lot of rich women having their hair done beautifully all the time, wearing nice clothes, etc. It's not just the money, it is because they have the time to take care of their feminine stuff. And it takes a lot of time. And, well, they like doing it for their men, because they are successful, confident, and probably not judgmental because they live in an abundance mindset. Now, before you call all women gold-diggers, this is not about the money. I repeat this is not about the money. Money is a store of energy, nothing more. You don't need to be rich, you just shouldn't be broke. Make enough to live comfortably with your woman. That's it on the money part. The rest of the environment depends on how you are. Are you a power plant giving lots of energy, and making it possible for your wife to be a bubbly, girly, woman, or do you delegate a ton of tasks to her because you are busy playing videogames? Does she have the time to go out with her female friends for coffee and be based in her femininity, or is she busy taking care of the home, finances, kids, and issues? Do you ravish her in bed with your masculine force, or is she on top all the time, and you're being fucked, instead of her? Did you ever ask yourself these questions?

You probably canceled the feminine environment she needs yourself. Don't worry, I made that mistake myself. It can be undone, but it takes work on your part. From now on, whenever your girl does something which isn't very feminine, or not to your liking, just ask yourself, "what environment am I creating for her here? Can she just be a girl? Or are there a lot of tasks which should be mine?"

FEMINISM

*Feminism is telling women that it is okay to
be a servant to a big company, but not okay to
be a servant to her husband and children.*

I kind of hate talking (or writing) about this topic because it just gives them more exposure, but you need to understand what this really is. Feminism is the idea that women are free when they serve a corporation, but they're slaves when they serve their husbands (and children). That's a bit harsh, I know. Originally, feminism was the idea of equal rights and opportunities. But, my friend. We long reached that. "What? How can you say something like that, you must be misogynist!" I mean, if you've come this far in the book, and are only now realizing that I am what would be considered "sexist" and "misogynistic pig" then I have bad news for you.

Anyway, we have equality of the sexes as much as it is possible. And this is the important caveat that feminists don't want to realize. As much as possible. Women are the ones bearing the children. It takes at least two years out of your life per child. And no matter how heavily you force your ideology down people's throats, this fact will not change. Is it unfair? Well, if that makes you feel better, then yes, it is unfair. Men have other challenges, but go ahead. The point is, unless you find a way to make men have babies, there will never be full equality for both sexes. I mean, there are tons of other reasons, like how men generally are more interested in leading than women, how men are more interested in gadgets than people, and how it's reverse for women. Which explains why so many men are in tech jobs, and women are nurses, and working in retail, etc. Feminists will then claim that these jobs are unfairly paid, and I actually agree with that. More blue-collar and retail jobs should get better pay. But this is not due to sexual prejudice. This is because of the nature of the market. If you design the newest iPhone App in Silicon Valley, you create value for millions or billions of people. If you serve twenty people at your local barbershop, then, well, you vanish in comparison. This doesn't say the value you created for these people is less. It's just less worldwide. And therefore you'll get paid less. Globalization.

Why do I talk about this? Because one big misconception feminists always bring up is the pay gap. It does exist, but NOT because of prejudice. Or maybe to a very, very small percentage which you will only reduce if you swing too heavy into the other extreme, which doesn't help anyone. I sometimes feel these people just want to reverse it completely, instead of focusing on actual equality. They want revenge for all the years where women were paid worse by prejudice. But seriously, that is utterly narcissistic and doesn't help society at all. The big part of the pay gap comes from motherhood, which can't be changed, different interests of the sexes and thus working in different jobs, and the basic difference in how they approach life. For example, men are generally more assertive. They go after what they want. Heavily, and by force. Women not so much. They are more empathetic. So men are generally more likely to ask for a pay raise. Just the asking. Not even negotiating. Just wanting to have more, whereas women are a bit more content with what they have.

This then is the time where they come in and talk about communism, or socialism, which is the same in a different dress. Yes, it is! The initiation is different, but the end result is the same. Because they both work on ideologies instead of the individual. And as long as you put people in groups, you will always end up with millions of dead people. Because you can play this game forever. Now women are oppressed. And black people. Then women working in retail. Then disabled women, then black disabled, women. Then ugly women. Then ugly, older women. Then black, disabled, ugly, remote living, older women. Whatever, you can make this so granular, that you will always find oppressors and oppressed. And as long as you bend society to the will of the minority, you will make it worse for the majority. Don't believe me? Just read any history book of when we tried communism. It is crystal clear how it ends, and why it's bad. The idea of it is flawed in its basis, but then again, feminists don't read history, because it renders their ideology pointless.

That said, the actual problem with feminists is that they don't want to be that kind of woman. They know what they would have to do to get from life what they want. But it's always easier to blame others than to change yourself. They don't realize that beta males have exactly the same issue. I was that guy. I blamed all of the women for going for jerks all the time. I did everything I could to please the woman, and she still didn't give me what I wanted. I knew, if I'd be a more manly guy, I would get it. But I praised myself with not being that kind of guy because from childhood I was told that this kind of masculinity is toxic. Just like women are told that submitting to a man is weak. Know what's weak? Screaming at others. Everyone can do it. But it takes real mental fortitude to change yourself. Even if you are not an outgoing feminist on Tweeter, growing up as a woman in recent decades made you either somewhat hate masculinity, because they steal your jobs, money, and opportunities (which is a lie), or you chose the other path of "sexual liberty" riding the cock carousel without thinking about the consequences. The point is, society gave up on true femininity and true feminism. True feminism is fighting for equal rights without calling any man who disagrees a misogynist. Feminism these days is trying to create a rift between both sexes. Women can do it all alone. I think the current COVID-19 pandemic showed what's really going on. It got really quiet all of a sudden in that camp. I guess all the feminists suddenly pulled out their dust-catching sundresses and were all feminine because they needed their men to help them. It is always in times of adversity when we see who we truly are. I hope some of them learned about it. And if, by pure accident, you are a woman reading this, be known that the media is trying to use you as a weapon. To push their narrative. Listen to your gut. Do you like men? Masculine men? Rugged, proper men? Who can defend you and your family? Help you get through times of adversity? Then why are you fighting it? And for the guys, stay away from these kinds of women, or if you want to have some fun, try debating them, but it's mostly pointless. Find a woman who loves men for what they are and realize how the media and general pop-culture is trying to paint the female goddess as utterly capable of ruling the world themselves. Up until there is a house fire, and you need some sexy firemen.

STRONG SUBMISSION

Submitting to a man takes an enormous amount of mental strength. Placing your life into the hands of another person is self-sacrificing and dangerous. For this, the woman seeks the strongest man she can find.

I talked so much shit on women and the archetypes, it is time to portray what positive femininity actually is. As always this answer can be found in the past. To be precise with the Spartans (again, I know). They were the only society of all the flourishing ancient Greek societies where women actually had some rights. Not only were they allowed to eat what the men ate, but they also were allowed outside and had somewhat revealing clothes. Nice, fancy dresses (for that time). And they received the same education or at least similar to the boys (except the fight training). Now, they didn't really have any possessions, but when the men were out in wars, they were the ones to take charge of the house and family property. So they at least temporarily had power. Sparta was the only state which did that, and it was also one of the most important and glorious states to ever surface the earth. But, the women weren't screeching feminists. They were very feminine, long hair, tried to keep their beauty, and where submissive to their husbands. They knew their place while still maintaining power. My point? A) You don't need to be an extreme feminist to get what you want. And B) Submissive doesn't mean doormat.

The spartan women were known to be tough ladies. As I said, they bathed their newborn in wine to see if they're strong enough to survive. They also had the reputation of birthing the strongest warriors because they were tough women. There is a famous quote from back then:

"Why are you Spartan women the only ones who can rule men?"

"Because we are also the only ones who give birth to men."

They ruled men? Not really. But since Spartan men were the majority of their time in barracks or in war, the women were charged with taking care of the household. They didn't really rule over men, they just had some power as well. As soon as the men got home, they gave away the power over the household to their husbands. This is the classic captain and first officer metaphor I keep telling guys. The man is the captain, and the woman the first officer. She is totally capable of taking charge temporarily, and you do listen to her input. But ultimately it is your decision. That said, nowhere in that whole situation was any of the ladies a brutal minger, insufferable cunt, or revolting to look at. Just like being a masculine man doesn't mean asshole. However, I am aware that this concept is way too nuanced for purple-haired pronoun-larpers on Tweeter. But maybe you'll learn something today. You can be a beautiful, strong, capable woman, but still be submissive and lovely to your husband. Those things aren't mutually exclusive. Spartan ladies managed that 2,000 years ago, so you clearly can do it today.

Now, don't get me wrong. Sparta was still an ancient Greek society. So the Spartan ideology still proclaimed the main role any woman had was to bear and raise healthy children. That is also why the spartan ladies had a huge emphasis on fitness. Because it was believed that a healthy, fit woman would bear healthy, strong children. Which we know is, in fact, true. Or to be precise, it increases chances significantly. Anyway, the main purpose of any woman today is still having and raising children. Triggered? Ask any woman who chose her career path over a family until her biological clock ran out. The overwhelming majority of them are almost suicidal sad and disappointed with their life choices. Now, it obviously isn't the only thing women are good for, but it is the core. It is our biology, we need them to survive. The woman gains her power through a proper husband. Women have a certain control when married to a capable man. Look at any first lady. They are generally feminine, submissive to their husbands, but still changing the world for good. This has always been the way how women exerted their power. Through influencing their husbands. Some more, some less. These days "strong, independent" women, however, try to mimic men 1:1. They literally try to become the man themselves, instead of trying to influence him. Which explains the masculine "women" we have today. If you apply masculine traits to get what you want, naturally, you will become more masculine.

Now, there is obviously more to this. Modern-day man is nowhere near the spartan warrior type of man. So, living through a weakling who plays videogames and nothing else isn't really "powerful" for the woman. And not every woman can be married to the president. But there are still capable men out there you can bring your feminine thoughts into consideration with. But if you are an insufferable cunt, you will only attract a weak loser who puts up with that. So what you should be doing as a woman, is to become a strong submissive woman, searching for a strong capable man. And for the guys, become a strong, capable man, and you will automatically attract the kind of woman you want. People always go out dating with the perfect person in mind, not realizing that whoever they are themselves, is exactly who they will attract.

Spartan women were also known for their notoriously short skirts, which had slits and revealed their thighs. The dresses were called the Dorian peplos. Along with being physically fit, and all of the young ladies wearing their hair long and open, these ladies were sexy. But it was a different kind of sexy. Unlike today where sexy is seeing nipples, or everything else but nipples, see-through clothes, and whaletails. Real, classy sexy is somewhat innocent and accidental. It keeps the fantasy up, along with something else. And while these women also were fit and somewhat powerful, it also meant they had self-esteem and knew their self-worth. Hence why great men went for them. Submitting to another person takes a lot of grit. Literally putting your whole life, and yourself in this person's hand. Hence why submissive wives are way stronger than any "independent" woman. They are aware of who they are, and they chose to gift their life into the hands of a great man. Submitting that way needs a lot of mental fortitude and self-esteem. Both of which, modern-day women don't get raised to have, sadly. So if you are the parent of a girl, raise her feminine, but also give her tasks to take care of. Raise her self-esteem, but make her know her place. It's not easy, but it will make her truly happy. Or have you ever seen a happy feminist? So, my friend, if you seek a future wife, make sure she has good self-esteem and isn't a straight man-hater, this way, you will gain a proper submissive wife. If you are the kind of man who deserves that.

FEMININE STRENGTH

*Many a man has fallen prey to the
feminine. Her sexual power is unmatched and
can crumble any man in seconds. A pure
feminine woman exerts so much power in her
environment, she needs to be met by a strong
masculine force.*

Another great trait of any proper woman is the strength that is inherited in pure femininity. No, it is not fighting coworkers, and screaming and yelling in court. That makes you an insufferable cunt. The true strength of a woman is how she forces her man to become the best he could be. Men constantly are annoyed by their nagging wives, and she's never happy and all that. Well, she isn't because you're just a shell of the man you were once. You need to see that differently, she is trying to force you to become more than you are. And I know, a lot of you think this is selfish from her because she just wants more money, but you're wrong. Women don't care more about money than anyone else. What they really care about is a strong, capable man. The brokest motherfuckers can have the most loving women. And the richest dudes can be fucked over by their women like there is no tomorrow. What a woman really is saying if she nags you, or shit-tests you, is, "please try to be more than you are now, it will make you happier." A woman's greatest gift is to support her man in his endeavors. Either by voicing concerns he didn't think about, by making life easier in the other regards, or by talking him into getting his shit together so he finally does what he says. You need to realize that if you say you want to do X, then this is something you really want. In your mind, you would enjoy having it, that's why you said it. Even if it just means fixing the damn boiler in the house which keeps making noises. But then you're too lazy, weak, or any other excuse to pull through. Your woman will then try to force you to do it with her feminine methods. But that isn't sorely to net her any benefits that might arise. It is to make you feel better because you wanted that!

Women are truly a great force in this. A lot of men hate the idea that they are forced to do something by their woman. It makes them feel inferior and I get it. But this only makes you feel inferior if you are in need of her validation to be someone. If you are man enough on your own, it doesn't matter if your woman "made you do something." Especially if it benefitted you. If anything, you two are on the same boat with things. You're just confused because she nags you. Yes, but women communicate very differently, they generally communicate covertly, she will only use direct words when all other methods of communication for her didn't work. If you just really don't get it!

Women are pleasers. I'll get to that in the sex chapter (obviously), but it is true anywhere else. Some more, some less, but their nature makes them nurturers, and pleasers to other people. They like helping kids, they like helping you. They want you to feel better. That's why they dress up for you because you enjoy it. That's why they cook for you because they want you to feel good. That's why they do all kinds of shit in bed for you because they want you to feel loved and satisfied. As you are reading this, you might think I am picturing a unicorn. Paradise City. Well, yes, this kind of woman has mostly been canceled in our culture. Because they've been told for years that it is bad to "serve" a man. It makes them weak and all that envious projection. I think I've been through this enough now. The point is. There are still some of these women out there. They are rare, as are proper men, right? So it's not the unicorn type, it's more the Waldo thingy, where you really need to look for it. But if you manage to find such a woman, and you've fixed yourself, and conquered yourself, then she will bring a kind of force into your life you haven't experienced. The masculine and the feminine work best if they both revel in their biological nature. Extreme poles on both ends. The strongest force is always between two opposing poles. If you're both very low on your biological extreme, then there isn't much force to play with. It's just "meh." However, if you are enjoying your positive masculinity, leadership, and embracing your energy, then your woman will submit herself to you, and into her feminine energy. And in turn, she will offer you her greatest gifts. Love, nurturing, warmth, life.

So stop being mad about her nagging and shit-testing you. See it for what it is, a trial to get you to be more than you are now. Because you want it, and she is helping you. Obviously, if she constantly is negative and has nothing feminine or graceful about her, you need to let go of that. It's pointless. But if she had (!) or sometimes still has grace, beauty, and femininity in her, then it is up to you to become what YOU want to be. With her help. Embrace yourself, and embrace what she is doing.

PART VI
SEX

When the opposite sexes finally come together, the energy released is so strong that it can create life out of the vastness of nothing. If you truly want to revel in your sexuality, you need to honor it as high as possible. In the end, it is the basis of what created us, and still does today.

This morning while scrolling through my Twitter feed I came across one of those "suicide girls," you know the type who thinks her body is a drywall to be painted with ink, posted something that made me shake my damn head. It was an image of her being almost naked, and her husband (!) jumping into the pic in the background with the weakest body language I've ever seen. The tweet said something along the lines of other men being insecure if they don't support their women having an OnlyFans (basically porn) account, and that her husband supports it.

This tweet had over 60,000 likes, and a lot of sex workers, sorry, I mean other private OnlyFans accounts, supporting the statement. Let's be real here for a second. The guy doesn't really "support" his wife being naked for thousands of other men. He is so weak, he needs the external validation other men give his wife, and therefore underlining his great choice in picking that woman. Which is a fallacy, she obviously picked him. And he just puts up with that, because he thinks he can't get any better woman which is probably true with that mindset. Now, usually, I wouldn't care about what other people do with their lives. But the problem displayed here is on a societal level, not just on the individual. This guy is a cuck. And cuckolding (finding joy in seeing someone else having sex or sexual relations with your woman) is a new thing. Well, not really, but back in the days, it was definitely rare, whereas today it has its own category on all porn sites and millions of videos of it. The reason why it exists is tenfold, and the reason why it is bad, as well. I'll get to that in a second.

Cuckolding exists because of free internet porn itself. As a man who has grown up with porn readily available everywhere, I noticed myself how I got trained to like watching other people have sex more than having it myself. I preferred positions and places where I could see myself from a third-person view better, like with mirrors. I was so focused on reenacting the scenes from the best porn clips I had seen. All porn is cuckolding porn because you train yourself to enjoy seeing other people having sex instead of enjoying it from your position. And the problem that arises from this, is that you start to enjoy butcher-sex. I call it that, because honestly, after quitting porn for years now, opening a porn website looks like a butchery to me. It's just body parts on display. You choose which part you like the most right now, and indulge in the "pleasure." Just like choosing the pork at the butchery for dinner later. It is a shallow version of human sexuality. Even animals have more meaningful sex. While they don't try to connect their souls (as far as we know), they do it to reproduce. Whereas humans these days have sex or watch porn to do what? There is nothing gained. They move their genitals and bodies around without any deeper meaning. Before you ask, yes, I do think sex for most people these days, is masturbating with someone else's body and therefore similar to just watching porn.

Apart from reproducing, sex is meant to be a connection between two people. It is loaded with emotion, comfort, uncomfort, joy, bonding, and deep love. That doesn't mean you only have hair-cuddling missionary sex. You can still bond while making her cheeks flap. The point is, that it is more than just genitals connecting. It is designed to make you come closest to the other person. Physically, as well as mentally. But this is never "taught" in porn. And most men (and women) get their sexual education from porn these days. Or at least from pop culture media which sort of has become the same. So they are taught to only care about body parts, the biggest boobs, the biggest dick, and that this makes for the best sex. But it doesn't. The best sex is had, when both are totally gone in the other person, even if it is just standard missionary. Too bad people these days have never experienced that. Otherwise, they wouldn't want to show their bodies to thousands of other men, because they already get enough from their man at home. And men wouldn't want other men to see their wife naked, because they have a sacred connection that can't be shared or "improved" with other people watching. Cheating is also not a thing because that connection is so strong, you don't need anyone else. Whereas when all you see is the body parts, it quickly becomes boring or repetitive. So you either go to crazy extremes like public cumwalks and all that, or you fuck someone else.

I don't even want to go into detail on how bad porn actually is. Especially for men. There is tons of evidence on that to find online. How it ruins your testosterone levels, your physique, your energy, your relationships. You'll find enough evidence about that on my blog. The point is, society has trained young people to indulge in meaningless sex which is the exact reason why divorce rates are sky high and we have a ton of weak males getting cucked. Nothing bonds two people like great, meaningful, deep sex. But the question is, apart from porn, how did we get to his point?

INDIRECT SHAMING

*Shaming people for their behavior is the
tool for the meta-rules and morals to be
enforced. You are free to do whatever you like,
but it has consequences. As long as there aren't
consequences to actions, we are again in Chaos.*

If you look at the past and how people reacted in regards to sex, it was somewhat embarrassing to talk about it in public. In some countries more, in some less. But it wasn't really an embarrassment, although there certainly is something embarrassing about being naked and aroused, it was more a certain withdrawal to talk about it. The reason being, that it is something between two people and that's where it should stay. This was enforced by religion. Forget the chastity, I talk about promiscuous women being shamed publicly. Sex working has always existed, but the prostitutes were always outcasts and not part of the general public. Any sex worker today will tell you that those were dark times. But from their point of view, of course. Hence why any sex worker today (like OnlyFans accounts) will heavily defend their "activities" because they know very well they have nothing to offer other than their very average bodies. And since they already made the choice to become sexual public property, and the internet remembers everything, there is no way of going back if shaming promiscuity would come back as a trend. They would literally be thrown in the pit with no way out. So their fight for their "rights" isn't from a position of freedom. It is out of fear.

The issue arises, because we are fighting for individuals at the cost of society. The fact that women don't get publicly shamed for fucking a ton of dudes, showing everything about them on Instagram and whatever, gives the impression to young ladies growing up that this is okay and a behavior to follow. The real crux is that men obviously support that behavior by giving these women attention (likes, follows, or even money). So they are reinforced in their beliefs. Which is weird because we make fun of these men. Even those sex-workers themselves always talk down on their clients. Obviously, because through this attention, the simps make those women into something higher just for being. They are just naked. Nothing any other women couldn't do. Yet, they pay them. This produces a certain form of entitlement in them. Totally undeserved, because honestly, there is nothing special about stripping in front of a camera.

However, even if it's not just digital attention, and you have a lot of men engaging in sexual intercourse with you, they still only do it for their quick relief. While the woman is searching for emotional connection and male attention, she only gets it if she puts out. But not from the same guy. Yes, I said, the basic wants for both sexes are attention for women and sex for men. This is the basis, but from this, you build upwards. A man who is searching for a wife, applies different filters than a man looking to get his dick wet. It doesn't matter how big your boobs are, how well your thighs are shaped when you are vetted for motherhood. Now, I am not saying we should start to stone women who have seen more than ten dicks. That's stupid. That would be direct shaming. What I say we (men) should do is indirect shaming to better society. By which I mean, stop giving thots so much attention. You don't even need to mouth the words that you don't want to marry such a woman, you just don't do it. If men go for proper women with manners and attitude, the problem solves itself.

People always give me shit that I put all the pressure on the men, but I told you before, responsibility = power. And I know, looking at the female body gives a great dopamine rush, so it's tough to stop scrolling Instagram thots. But if you want a proper wife who admires you, follows your lead and likes having sex with you instead of drip-feeding it, you need to stop giving those digital asses attention and lead yourself. Through this indirect shaming of women's behavior, men would be able to raise more proper women you can marry. Remember, the feminine is chaos (emotional), the masculine is order (rational). So, as long as you let everything slip what the feminine is doing, you will create a society of chaos. And we already see what this brought us. Genderfluid people, people being arrested for not addressing them with their made-up pronouns, and planned parenthood literally murdering millions of people because it's "easy." The current, dark state of society is because we don't put boundaries on bad behavior. This is true on your relationship level, as well as on a societal level.

Now, you might think I am a misogynist for wanting to shame women. That's where you're wrong kiddo. I think we should also shame men for being weak losers. Indirectly. It's hard to put this on women, because the beta orbiter type is very beneficial to her as a source of passive income, so I would (again...) put this on the men. The friends. Your pals. Good friends don't let buddies fall for mediocrity. More men need to stand up and tell their buddies that they are making bad decisions that weaken their life, and themselves. Be it with women, monetary, or business. You should absolutely have an inner circle of maybe five guys, with which you sit together each week and talk about your deeper life. You want answers from external bystanders if what you are doing seems logical from the outside. Of course, not everyone knows the details, and you shouldn't just do what they say, but you definitely should take their opinions into account.

Back in the days, men would've been ashamed to take $1,200 bucks from the government to fix their life (like in the current COVID-19 pandemic). Because it directly tells them they fucked up. Made bad life decisions, so they can't even bridge a temporarily bad economy. These days, simps are complaining it is not enough money. Free money! Not enough! This kind of weak-ass behavior is shameful and that's how it should be called out. In the case of men, some direct shaming would work well, because we sometimes need to be hit on the head with a hammer to finally understand the point. And while you're at it, shame your bros for spending money on average-looking "suicide girls" on OnlyFans.

RAPE CULTURE

If you water down the meaning of words,
you hurt every person that got hit by its
original meaning the worst. And if you start to
water down most heavy words, you end up
with an easy to ruin society.

While I write this there is a clip trending in Germany from two comedians who tried to raise awareness about sexual harassment. The clip opened with women being sent unsolicited dick-pics, and some "I would bang her" comments on Youtube. You know what made dick pics possible or a thing? The sexual revolution. We praise it as something good and progressive that women get to fuck around as much as they like, bitch control pills, show as much skin as they like, without consequences, but it is a fallacy. Because if it is totally normal for any woman to show a ton of cleavage or butt pics on Instagram, then you lower the barrier for sexual encounters. Naturally. Everything becomes sexualized, even if you just open Instagram. Hell, every ad, every TV show, every movie has tons of nudity and literal sex-scenes. And due to the fact that most men grow up with their sexual education through porn, and even tons of amateur porn, where normal girls do this voluntarily, they learn that just dropping yer pants will make her eyes widen and immediately wet like the niagara falls.

Think about it. If you grow up somewhat socially distanced, because you had no proper masculine figures in your life - like most men these days - you have a tough time working with the feminine energy. So all you learn about sex is from porn which is readily available everywhere. You then see average girls from school, flaunting themselves on Instagram or OnlyFans. Naturally, you would think this is how women operate. Through the visual.

Especially if nobody (like me) tells you how it really is. Proper men never send dick pics. They get nudes without showing themselves at all. The dick pic is really the weak man's approach.

However, great man or weak man, we all judge people by the cover. Women do it, too. Everyone does. If you have to evaluate each person anew every time you meet them, that would be one hell of a mental task. And to save energy, as a survival instinct, we judge people by their appearance and within the first seconds of meeting them. So if you are half-naked on your Instagram pics, I will put you in the drawer under "promiscuous." This might be the only thing in this book that I actually do blame on the women. They hate hearing that, but the way you dress, the things you do with your body, have consequences. If you dress promiscuously, you will naturally be perceived as promiscuous. I mean, the term implies it? If a man dresses in a tailored suit, he will automatically be perceived as successful, or confident. If you wear functional body armor, people think you're a rugged soldier. If you dress homeless, people think you're homeless. If you wear glasses, people think you are intelligent. Now, none of this might be true, I agree. But it still displays exactly that. It helps you to categorize someone quickly. And I know, at this point the sex-workers will come in and argue that this is "shallow" and you should put more effort in judging people accordingly. Which is funny, because in 90% of the cases, the perception you have of the person is actually correct. Stereotypes exist for a reason. They weren't invented by someone tossing a coin and thinking, "this should be pretty accurate." They came about because the majority of the people put in that stereotype are like that. Again, not everybody. And not every woman wearing a short skirt is also fucking a ton of dudes, or has nothing else to offer. But if it applies to the overwhelming majority, then I am taking that chance of putting you in that drawer. Everyone does.

That said, all of this created this rape culture. We introduced words like "eye-rape" and watered down the meaning of this very loaded word so much, that any woman claiming to be sexually harassed these days will be questioned heavily. Maybe not publicly, but definitely in people's mind. If I see one of those harpies on Twitter saying she got "eye-raped" and sexually harassed somewhere outside, I am really wondering if it really wasn't just some dude checking her out. And sorry, looking at another person is not rape! Not even eye-rape!

The reason this came about is because emotional and loaded words like rape work well on the internet and in headlines. I know this because I run a blog, and the articles with the most emotional words in the headline or snippet work the best. This is because it triggers our emotional part of the brain and we're more inclined to read more about that story to either feel empathy or be outraged. This is why things like rape and sexual harassment got so watered down. Some women just want male attention and therefore dress skimpy. However, she then gets attention from the weak simp instead of the hot dude, and suddenly she got eye-raped. The issue is, that this makes it harder for any woman that actually got raped or sexually harassed to make her case. Because you sort of stop believing in these stories. And there are still men (yes, men as well!) and women who get sexually harassed a lot. And it's not because they're wearing the tightest skirts. It's because some men are just assholes. Yes. That doesn't mean all men are.

And this always gets sold under the "what kind of society do we live in where I can't wear what I want?" I'm sorry. I cannot wear whatever I want, either. I am now gonna buy pants where my balls hang out freely, because the sun on my balls actually increases testosterone production, so I'll be more healthy. No, I can't do that because it displays that my balls are the thing I care for the most. But even if it wasn't, showing my balls to everyone lowers my value, doesn't it? You immediately think of me as weird. And you would be right. We never could "wear what we want" in history, ever. For good reason. Or rather, we can wear what we want, but there are consequences to it. As there are to every action you do. You are free to wear a skirt so short I can see your cheeks, but be sure that you radiate that the best thing you can offer is your sexuality. Which is true for many women these days. Just like most men bring nothing to the table but their salary, most women bring nothing to the table but their reproductive organs. They can't cook, they can't take care of children, or even pets, can't take care of their beauty (which I will get to, soon), hell, all they do is party and get boozed up. Just like the men can't fight, can't lift, can't lead, can't be decisive. It all comes down to sex. Shallow sex. This is what "connects" both genders these days. And if that is all you have, naturally, you will display a lot of it. Because you have no other way of drawing people towards you.

And then, since you grow up with so much sex around you, it is natural for you as a woman to show skin. Because everybody does. But then you are surprised why all men just want to fuck you and don't call back after the first romping session. Well, what you radiate is what you get. If you radiate your sex-appeal, naturally men are interested in sex. If you radiate your femininity in a cute sundress, and being fun to be around instead of an insufferable cunt, then he is more likely to see a wife in you than a fuck-toy. Women will never understand how easily men can discern this. We can have sex without emotions, no problem. Relief ourselves, next. This is totally possible for most men. In femininity and its display, we see more than just sex. That's when we see a warmth, a glow, and a proper mother for future children. And sex, of course. But honestly, if you don't want to be "eye-raped" just don't walk around half-naked and virtually radiate you have nothing else to offer. Men are wired like that, and you won't change millions of years of biology with your ideology. It's the same problem we always have. Instead of changing yourself to change the outcome, you try to change everyone else. Doesn't work like that. But I know it's easier to send that Tweet, instead of rethinking your own decisions.

And the real issue for society is that men just let it slide. The rape-accusations. It wasn't rape. You should call her out for such bullshit. You were checking her out, which is totally fine if you can almost see her nipples. Nothing wrong with that. If she doesn't like it, she needs to dress differently, or be aware that sometimes a dude might check her out which is not to her liking. That doesn't mean he will immediately rape her. Hell, it's an indication of interest. If you look at a woman, she is attractive to you. How in the world did we end up in a society where this is called out as being bad? And no, if you dress sexy, that doesn't mean there will be 100 men cat-calling you. That's just made-up bullshit. Some might, see it as a compliment. They like your body, nothing wrong with that.

But because this was pushed so heavily we're now constantly talking about consent. You need to make sure she really likes what you're doing. Which is totally backward to biology and what women really want deep down. She wants to be taken by a strong man. A man who takes her although she says a token "no." It is her nature. Don't believe me? Look at how well your sex-life is going with never pushing through, and doing everything she says. And look at the men who do it differently. How come they always get the hot women? Because she only wants this from a proper man, a strong man, who has his shit together, is grounded in his masculinity, and is interesting. Which is why the eye-rape is probably even a thing. Remember back in the 1950s where each man was a real man. Unlike today. Women were totally fine being checked out, because most men would've actually been a great catch for them. Not so much these days where everyone checking you out is a weakling. So while I blame the women for dressing so open-hearted and thus being surprised they get called out, I also blame the men. If you are a decent man, you won't have issues with checking out a hottie. She'll like it.

So we end up with a society where any woman being cat-called was raped because of weak men. And any woman who really got raped is being questioned about it. Is that a society you want? On top of that, we have women who have nothing to offer but their bodies, and men who offer nothing but their money and a bit of weak male attention. If so. This is the sex our sexes have. Shallow, irrelevant, abundant and thus meaningless, and also, loaded with possible accusations. Brave new world.

LINGERIE

Anything worthwhile takes time. If you
don't put the time into foreplay, enjoying her
body and yours, you're merely connecting your
genitals. Nothing more.

If you look back to the 80s and 90s, lingerie was the shit. Not just cool lacy panties. Stockings, suspenders, and all that. Playful and almost complicated underwear. That time frame is also where femininity peaked for women. The most feminine, bubbly, and naturally beautiful women were from that age. There is a coincidence. Because lingerie isn't just made to make you horny. Extravagant lingerie like those corsets and stockings are actually a hindrance to get into her, right? So why did we bother with this? Simple. We didn't just want to stick it in, we wanted to make it a journey. Special lingerie is mostly for the foreplay. Not for the act itself. But since foreplay these days is literally just watching porn together, this isn't relevant anymore. Lingerie turns a woman into more than she is. It is designed to underline the beauty she already possesses. Lingerie can't make a woman beautiful or sexy. It can only increase what she already has. It reveals her true sex-appeal. If you look at obese women in lingerie, it doesn't make them hotter (unless you are into big girls), whereas a girl you already enjoy seeing naked, becomes 100x more attractive in nice lingerie. It unleashes her inner beauty. And why is that? Because she feels sexier in it. It amplifies her radiating her femininity and sex-appeal. Some women say they wear lingerie for themselves, not for their man, and it is correct. She feels sexier. Partly, because she knows that you like it, but partly because she knows, she looks fucking sexy now. And in turn, she will be more into it, you enjoy her being more into it, everybody wins.

However, if I talk to men these days, a lot of them voice that they don't need this at all, they want their girls naked to "get to it." Or it's "too much work to get it off" and "it's in the way." Reading these answers, you know exactly what's the issue at hand. They want to get it over with. They don't care about the connection, they just want to shoot their load. Get the dick hard, put it into her, monotone thrusting for 5 minutes, done. Fall asleep. Women hate this, because it sucks. But men do too, they just don't know. It's the reason they try to fill their inner void by filling lots of voids. That sex is meaningless and irrelevant. It doesn't touch your soul. And thus they try to find that in tons of other women.

Now I am not saying there is anything wrong with testing your horn(s) on lots of women. You do you. But remember that you are searching for something deeper. And other women won't fix that. Lingerie alone won't fix it, either. But it is a way to get closer to it. Not only does it give your woman more feminine grace, which is what you really want (yes, you do, stop denying it), it will improve your sex-life. Because you spend time admiring her body, touching it, feeling it. You have time to look into her eyes. Like, really look into them, connecting with her soul, instead of just connecting with her pussy. And trust me, if you connected with her soul, her pussy will be way wetter and hotter for you.

That said, since this society primed women to be more and more "open-hearted" and promiscuous, you see a lot of them skipping lingerie on their own altogether. There is that bra-free movement, which apparently is a movement of freedom for women to not having to wear a bra. I mean, this was never a thing. They never had to. They decided to do because it's more comfortable, and to stop them from sagging at the age of 25. So nowadays, you have these women who don't even want to put the effort to put on something nice, because they think it is for you. They think, they only do that for you, because you enjoy it. And feminism told them, doing anything for a man is toxic and reducing her standing as a woman. Not only is that wrong (I think we covered feminism at length), but it's also the wrong reason. As I said, lingerie is designed for her. It's tough to get this into women's heads these days because they've been so conditioned. And, well, since they all eat wrong, smoke, and drink alcohol like my grandfather never could, they don't even like their own, chubby bodies. Which I guess is understandable, but it also means, that the lingerie won't work for them. Again, it only underlines the existing beauty and grace. If she doesn't like her body at all, lingerie will only make it worse.

However, if your woman is healthy, and eats properly (like you do I hope), you can ask her to put things on. And if she does, don't just rip it off, that's a waste. Embrace it, get yourself into foreplay. But don't make the mistake most men do and make foreplay about her, "because women like that." Learn to enjoy it yourself. Discover her deeper than just the soft-skinned surface. Get into her deeper than just the length of your dick. Get into her eyes, her soul, her very being. David Deida, who wrote the book, "The way of the superior man" which I would highly recommend said, "you penetrate the world like you penetrate your woman." If you only scratch the surface, you will only get the basics from the world, or the universe. If you really go deep into her, you will also go deep into the world. Make sex more than just shooting your load. Make it a connection between you two, and see your life thrive.

SEXUAL STRATEGY

Both sexes sexual strategies are opposite to
each other. Just like the sexes itself. If you want
to maximize your existence with your partner,
you need to find ways to incorporate their
sexual strategies in everyday life.

If you are following my blog or me, you are aware of the actual deeper sexual dynamics between men and women. Men are polygamous, which means, biologically, they try to fertilize as many women as possible. Whereas women are hypergamous, which means they try to get fertilized by the best mate possible, but rarely. As with anything, if you want to know if such things are true, just look at biology. A man can reproduce in five minutes or more (depending on your skills...) and then he is done. He can proceed with his life and move on. A woman however, if she gets pregnant from one man and thus reproduced, she now has nine months at least where her life is very different. Not only is she less attractive for other mates, but she also becomes pretty vulnerable. Sickness, moveability of her body, other pregnancy problems. And unless she ditches her child right after, she now has the burden of the child for many years. So naturally, it would make sense for the woman to be very sure who she reproduces with. Not so much for the lads. We can just make a kid and leave. By the way, this is just the biological standpoint, there are obviously other important factors, especially in today's society. However, these biological drives are deeply ingrained in us, and therefore should be noted. We can decide to consciously ignore them to a certain degree, or even our whole life, but they will always be looming, which is the topic of this chapter.

Stick to your damn biology. I am not saying men should freely fuck around. Obviously. I am a married father, and I stick to my wife voluntarily, despite writing these words. My point is this, if you want to have a healthy sex-life, and therefore a healthy relationship and marriage, you need to embrace your biology in your everyday life and sex. If we accept the hypergamous and polygamous natures of both sexes, it is necessary that men, at least visually, gets to have sex with different women or different visuals. Which means, lingerie, positions, places, and even roleplay. We can totally have a fulfilled polygamous sex-life with one woman. See, the biological drives are pretty animalistic, and basic. Which is why porn works. The brain, or rather the limbic system part of it cannot discern between a sexual act in front of you while literally having it, and a sexual act just seen on a screen. It still triggers arousal and the drive for reproduction. However, it is lacking the touching of another person's skin, the comfort and uncomfort of sex, and the bonding with said person. Which is also why porn mostly works on men. We are visual. The visual triggers are enough for us. When my wife bends over while cleaning the room and I see through her pants, I am ready. I can go right here and there. Which is what porn is. See a sexual image, get off. That is how men work. Our arousal is spontaneous. However, for women, their desire is responsive. They get aroused when a man sexually courts them. Women rarely have a spontaneous desire. It happens, but rarely. You need to woo them with words, behavior, and display of confidence, that's what turns them on. Which porn has none of that. Which is hypergamy again. They want to be desired by the most fittest, and most Alpha males to make sure their reproduction and potential time investment of nine months or more are worth the sexual encounter.

So what to learn from this? Simple. If you want to keep your sex-life up, you need to be a proper man, and you need to display this when engaging your wife in sex. Which means, be confident, be fit, pass her shit-tests, and lead her. Like a true man does it. And for the ladies, be a different kind of woman every time. Lingerie, costumes, be open to new positions and places. However, since the masculine is the leader, all of this is usually initiated by the man. And if she can let herself fully go in your masculinity, because you are a true catch to her basic instinct, she will do all these things for you, because the potential of mating with such a great man outweighs second thoughts. So guys, re-read the manliness chapters, become that dude and embrace your deeper biology.

That said, the reason I bring this up in this culture, is because we have ditched our basic biology. Often times I see men say they would like their women to initiate more. Or even that women approach in a bar if they're interested. This is horseshit. It just displays a weak male. And a man who has no idea how to read female cues, probably because he didn't have a father who told him that (like me). If a woman has to be overt about her intentions, she has to do that because all other methods of her covert communication didn't work. It is her last resort, and she hates that. Because it is masculine. She needs to ditch her feminine core to do that. Women don't like to communicate that way. And if even she approaches you directly in a bar, she hates doing it. And is probably desperate. But even if it ends in mating, she ultimately resents the fact that you didn't have the balls to approach a woman, and you are thus lacking masculine traits.

Skipping our basic biology only ever works short-term. The longer you are in an un-biological relationship, the higher the chances it will fail. This is true, not just in romantic relationships. Women and men aren't meant to be friends. The polarity between the genders will always be reason for tension. And if it works longer, then the reasons are because both are not deeply in their masculinity and femininity ingrained. If he is pretty feminine, and she is pretty masculine, then it might work. See "the gay best friend." Now, David Deida from The way of the superior man said, that relationships can work when the man is feminine, and the woman masculine, as long as both keep the polarity between each other up. Personally, I disagree with that. Or rather, he is right about the polarity, but if you are not true to your biology, there will always be issues. Over the long run, the feminine male will notice problems. Inner issues he can't address properly. The desire to lead and be around guys, especially when he grows older. And the masculine female will hear a calling of being submissive every now and then and wanting to submit to a proper male.

Again, it might work for a certain while, but long-term, after the initial butterflies settle, and a certain routine comes into life, we tend to fall into autopilot on ourselves. And on autopilot, we work to our biology. Remember, the decision to not be close to your nature was conscious. Either through external conditioning (i.e. society, growing up in a certain environment) or because you decided to do so. However, you never decided to be a man or a woman when you were born. This is your destiny, and it will always come back. So the easiest way to not deal with those internal conflicts years after being married (if you consider yourself close to your nature or not) is to be closer to it voluntarily. Accept who you were born as. Yes, you can switch genders these days, but it is only on the surface. Deep down, you will always know who you were when you were born. This will always haunt you. So, men, learn to lead in real life. Be confident, have a mission, be masculine. And ladies, learn to submit to a proper man, learn how to be a woman, be nurturing, and give warmth. Nobody likes an insufferable cunt (the Karen archetype), and nobody likes a weak male (the simp). Society will tell you otherwise, but they canceled biology long ago.

PART VII
BEAUTY

The man who has incorporated and chiseled his own beauty, is the man who can adore the beauty in other things. A human's inherent drive is to follow beauty. A society ignoring that fact will naturally become very ugly, not just from its appearance. Also, from within.

Are you familiar with brutalism? That architectural "style" came over the United States in the 1950s and was probably the most atrocious idea mankind has ever had towards their buildings, and literally the basis of nature. Look at it:

It's just a grey block. I can't even fathom what the people were smoking back then. The only explanation I have is (again) people wanted to be "different." That unending drive to just be different for the sake of it. Just because you're special, doesn't mean you're awesome. Yes, I repeat myself. We did give up on beautiful buildings and thus having beauty around as at any given time. Remember the olden days:

Where would you rather be around? Just walking past the two buildings while you mind your business? Which one touches your soul? Which one has a soul? I know you might be wandering through your day, totally sucked into your Smartphone and you don't even notice these things. Which is probably another reason why we actually build houses and buildings these days just "that'll do." Nobody sees it anyway, no point in putting in any effort, right? Maybe that's not the cause, but the effect? I don't know about you, but if I were walking through a city with beautiful buildings, I wouldn't need to stare into my phone all the time.

But why is beauty so important that I spend a whole chapter lamenting about it? Beauty is power. It is in our nature to choose the most beautiful thing to get. Do you pick the most beautiful flower from the garden or the one almost rotten away? Do you choose the most beautiful woman you can score, or the brutal minger? Do you buy a good-looking car (if you can afford it), or the ugly Fiat Multipla? Do you enjoy the beautifully prepared food or food from a metal can? Need any more examples? Beauty IS power because beauty gets chosen over ugliness. Always. In any regard.

Beautiful people have it easier in life. People hate that fact, but it's true. Not just women when being chosen as a partner, men as well. The good looking, masculine dude has it not only easier with women, but also with business, friends, opportunities, and success. And ugly people try so hard to kill off this fact. Look at any feminist, or transgender person. There really isn't anything beautiful about them. It's not even "traditional" values of beauty, they just radiate ugliness, by being constantly negative, intentionally asymmetric in their appearance, and overall behavior. Why would you want to be around such a person? And it's not like these people are just naturally ugly and therefore "tough luck" and they rebel. No, a lot of times, they were once beautiful or at least decent looking people. Which could've easily raised their objective beauty value if they put some effort in their appearance. Man and woman alike. But it's always easier to blame others, and trying to change others, even if it is a whole society, than to change yourself. A positive feedback loop of other voluntary ugly people helps to reinforce that.

And that is how society gave up on beauty. And is still in the process of doing so. Maybe I should say the Media gave up on it. Because even though you are spoon-fed with those ugly people and their weird message, all day, you will still enjoy a muscular guy in bed, or a classic feminine body to reproduce. And the reason? Biology doesn't care. Sex is the closest we ever get to our deepest biology. As the Rational Male said, desire cannot be negotiated. Either you are attracted to someone or you're not. And the overwhelming majority of men still want traditional looking women with symmetric faces, long hair, wide hips, a round ass, and so on. Just like women still prefer a guy with visible muscles, who is strong, confident, and Alpha. Both genders just tend to settle for less these days more than ever. Partly, because society keeps telling you "you can't have everything" and you suck it up, and partly because you literally have no self-esteem to believe you could have more beauty in your life. And we see the implications in sexless marriages. The men get "dad-bods" and do nothing but watch football and chug 15 beers. And in turn, the women cut off their hair, because long hair is intensive to take care of, and "if he doesn't put in the effort, why would I?" plus putting on weight with a ton of sugar and excusing this self-deteriorating behavior with "we're married, we have kids, it's just how it is."

So not only do people give up on keeping their beauty, which is way easier than regaining it, if that is even possible, they also give up on themselves. And the result? No sex. As I said before, sex is the closest to your deepest biology. If the other person just doesn't look like a good salesperson for their genders' genetic material, your biology is not interested. It's like the dude at the door trying to sell you a new fancy suit. If he is wearing a badly fitted, dirty suit, why would you buy from him? And so, if your man or woman is trying to sell you their genes, because that is what sex in your hindbrain comes down to, you're not willing to do it if they don't represent at least the minimum effort of that gender. That's why I keep preaching to men that if the sex stopped in their marriage, your first issue to tackle is your goddamn dad-bod. Visually become a man again. Even if you're weak in other parts, this alone can rekindle it. And get your lady to stop smoking, and eat healthy. You do that by leading yourself, and showing that it has benefits to be healthy. Since I started eating more healthy and exercising, my wife followed suit voluntarily. I didn't even ask her. She just did it. Or asked me how to do it or why. Remember the natural operation of both sexes, leader and follower. If you want a beautiful, fit wife, you need to be a beautiful, fit husband.

FEMALE BEAUTY

A man can quickly fall for a woman's
beauty. But he needs to be aware that there are
two kinds of it. One will trigger your
animalistic desires, and one will trigger your
poetic love.

When a woman grows up, she will eventually notice that her body inherits a lot of power over other people. Man and woman alike. Well, unless she's born as Shrek, and she ruins her beauty with boozing each weekend, smoking, and killing her inherent vibe with riding a ton of dudes. If she just grows up a decent girl, she will notice that her feminine beauty has an insane draw to it. The problem is, due to the porn-addict generation, we're looking at the wrong things here. That girl with 9 million followers on Instagram only posting images of her butt has her thinking that this is what men want. And that this is the beauty-idol for any woman. And while a fertile butt is nice to look at, she would be very wrong with that. Paradoxically, female beauty can't be seen but is also visible. Huh?

Look, there is objective beauty, which we measure in ratios of hips to waist, symmetricity of the face, and all that. But this is very shallow. It works for porn and hooking up in this culture, but deeper beauty, the one that has real power, comes from within and shines outward. You probably keep hearing this from the body positivity movement, where obese people keep excusing their lazy minds with that. But the feminine beauty from within is a symbiont between the body and the soul. And that's why it is seen in the eyes. Compare the two images.

The one on the left probably has millions of followers on Instagram, praising her body-parts, and that's it. The one on the right probably has tons of men actually loving her. You could also make a distinction between "hotness" and "beauty." The left one is hot. It triggers the right receptors in the male brain, so they want to copulate. Hence why men shower her with attention, because they just want to stick it in there. The one on the right radiates beauty. She is beautiful. A man still wants to have sex with her (obviously), but he also wants more. He wants to have kids with her because she radiates femininity. A deeper beauty that the girl on the left can't provide. People keep saying that girls like the one on the left are "dumb," but they're not. They're just shallow. They learned that their body has a certain power over men, and since women work on attention, she is sort of addicted to it. Her body is her weapon, her source of the attention-dopamine she gets from men. This has been immensely multiplied since we have Instagram. Women sell their souls for the cheap attention from Filtergram. And since pretty much any man these days watches porn, all he sees in a woman, are her body parts. I have watched porn years ago. Obviously, every man did and still does. But as soon as I quit (which was hard, PUN intended), I started to be attracted to a different kind of woman. The one on the right. Nowadays, the left girl is somewhat revolting to me. It is hard to describe, but there is nothing that draws me to her. It may be the connection to porn. Porn is for men what Instagram is for women. Women work on attention. Men on visuals. Both give exactly that, but a very shallow version of it. That might be the reason why she does nothing for me. The girl on the right though is natural. There is more to her than just her body. She radiates something. Obviously, she also posts on Instagram, but it's more than just ass pics. There is more depth to it. And that is part of the female beauty.

Men are explorers, we want to dive into mysteries and unravel them. And feminine beauty offers that. There will always be a certain draw to it, which is hard to describe. But it is always silent. Which brings me to Karen. You know the archetype of the Karen, right? Basically an insufferable cunt. Sorry for any girl that's called Karen, although it's quite funny that this recently has been called "oppressing to all Karens." It's a damn meme, calm your tits. Anyway, the Karen is the kind of woman who cut her beautiful long-hair for a "modern" but also ugly look. But that's just one part, the more important part is she is constantly cited because she wants to "speak to the manager." You know, the kind of woman at the store in line who is just really annoying, makes everyone's day worse with all that negative energy. This kind of woman radiates zero femininity. You know it deep down. Any woman knows it as well. There is just something very masculine about that kind of act. True feminine beauty is silent. She works with cues, looks, subtle hints. Feminine beauty has something somewhat childish. That's also why men always go for younger women. Sometimes very young. It's not that they like the hot young bodies (well, maybe a bit), but the big part is that the femininity in those girls radiates stronger. Because they are still closer to their youth, the child in them is still there. Wonder why the sexy school-girl, sexy cinderella, and braids are such a thing in bed? They have a girly vibe. See, as a man, you have enough issues to take care of. Being with a feminine woman somewhat releases you of it. You can have fun with her. She is bubbly and funny to be around. That's what we seek. This is inherently childish. And that is exactly what she kills off if she tries to be a career woman because she will need to be an adult at all times. Also if she fucks a ton of dudes, because a girl doesn't do that. She loses that girly innocence.

Now, obviously, we men still want to ravish the shit out of that girly, youthful beauty in bed. Of course. But it is different to do it with one man because there is a connection. Her beauty will stay and even flourish afterward. Whereas with multiple men it slowly fades. Also, as soon as she has kids, she obviously needs to mature a certain bit. Because she now has other kids to take care of. But this doesn't necessarily mean it kills of her feminine, girly vibe. For a woman, her best gift is to keep that girly vibe all her life. I know, corporations, cosmopolitan, and commilitones will tell her she needs to "grow up." But if she wants to have a flourishing relationship with a decent man, she needs to preserve that youth. That is what keeps us men. Well, us proper men. Her objective beauty, coupled with her radiating femininity is what attracts us. But what keeps us, is if she is fun to be around. And if your woman is that Karen-Archetype, then chances are high that you, as a man, are a simp, who just accepts what he has instead of going for something he wants.

MALE BEAUTY

Man's beauty comes later in life but lasts
longer than the female. A man incorporating
his strength, confidence, and aggression in his
visual appearance will have no issues
conquering the world, women, and his own life.

I am pretty sure, some "journalist" will read this chapter and call me gay for being so hellbent on male beauty. Well, you know the meme, "Is being a man gay? Because, as a man, you're literally inside a man's body, and that sounds pretty fucking gay to me." Anyway, our culture has canceled male beauty. These days, men have "dad bods" and we're told that women actually like that. Even the mannequins in stores now have a belly, which sort of depicts how far this society has fallen. If we look back to ancient Greece (again), we will find hundreds of statues, images, and descriptions of ripped, jacked, and strong men.

This is the kind of male physique you see everywhere from back then. And it wasn't because people were starving and we have it so much better now. If you don't have food, you can't build muscle. You might be thin, but not muscular. These guys had enough food, they trained every day, and they trained outside which made these bodies possible. These days, a man's training consists of sitting in front of a computer, stuffing high carbohydrate foods in his mouth, not moving all day, not getting any sunlight. These men grow fat and resentful. Why resentful? Because they never get to experience the confidence, and glory of being able to change the world by pure physical strength of their body. And, well, because no woman likes to suck a sweaty, fat man. I mean, it's just what it is. So you end up unable to move properly, low energy, low testosterone, no sex, no power, and no confidence. And you're surprised why you're so negative and resentful at all times?

What does this have to do with beauty? Well, just like sex, and beauty for women, so, too, is the beauty for men way deeper than just a chiseled body. Ever since I fixed my diet and my gym routine, and actually got lean and muscular, my mindset shifted completely. I talked about entrepreneurship and success in regards to this in an earlier chapter, but this is about confidence. Male beauty, just like female beauty, is what you radiate. The vibe you give off. You could be jacked as hell, but if you're a negative nancy, nobody wants to be around you (although this would be rare because you wouldn't be jacked with that mindset). You know, you mastered the gym, you got the best out of your genetic material. You literally became the best physical version of yourself. You accomplished something in real-life. Not a meaningless achievement on your Xbox. And because of this, you are confident. You are a man in reality. You know what you're capable of, and this radiates through your vibe. People see quite literally what you're capable of, and that is why I mentioned earlier that I judge people by their appearance. Well, everybody does, really.

However, the body positivity movement, and pretty much any lazy, obese person, worked hard to stop people from judging appearance. Because they didn't want to hear that. I get that if someone tells you you're a fuck-up, that is never nice to hear. But nice to hear things never make you grow. Pain is what makes you grow. Suffering, overcoming obstacles. A lean, healthy body is not gained by chilling around. It takes effort, sweat, and pain. But since this society raised a ton of weaklings, naturally we would rather choose not to offend people, instead of telling them how to actually enjoy themselves and not be bitter about what they very well know is wrong with them. It's always funny to me when obese people say they like their bodies. No, they don't. They have a ton of issues, health problems, can't move properly, no energy, and die almost immediately if a predator is around. They rationalize and justify their bullshit to not accept the fact that they would need to change something about themselves to get more out of life.

And here we are at my point, I think we should come back to judge men more heavily on their appearance. Beauty is power which I finally will get to in the next chapter, and men need power to achieve anything in their life. Most of you have that power within you, you just neglect it so heavily. You accept becoming fat at 30, because life's over, right? Well, if you peaked in high-school I got bad news for you. 60 years of misery are waiting.

Women won't tell you what they really think about your body. Only in the last minute, basically. As I said, before, women communicate covertly. The medium IS the message. So if she doesn't want to have sex with you regularly, then THIS is your message that something is wrong. And if you're obese, sweaty, and can't move, I would start there. Because it's the most obvious solution. And, yes, women will say, they don't care much about appearance, and you will see Flavio Briatore, a pretty ugly, fat man with the hottest models and think, you don't need to put in the work. But this man is highly successful, an Alpha, and a player. This works, but only short-term. If you want a long-term solution, you need to get back (again) to biology. What you display to your woman physically, is what her hindbrain judges for reproduction. Just like you judge her appearance for your reproduction. And if you look like a Greek god or Gigachad below here, well, she'll have a hard time resisting that.

Now, obviously not everyone has his genes to get such a magnificent full, and strong beard. But you can absolutely maximize what you have by sculpting your body. And he is certainly something to strive towards. However, this man itself is another phenomenon of this culture. He has become a meme called Gigachad. You know, chad is the Alpha kind of guy, and he, well, is Giga the Alpha. And naturally, weak PC gaming culture and incels are making fun of his photoshoot images, because they try to cope with their own shortcomings by making him look comically, or ludicrous. This is always a coping mechanism by weak people. Instead of seeing such a person as a symbol, idol, or godlike image to strive towards, they try to make fun of it to justify their own weakness. This is what our society has done at large. Bodies like that are almost always made fun of. They're "gym-bros" and because they're on steroids and all that, they have small balls and are stupid. That is the narrative. Just like any very beautiful woman "has nothing else to offer."

The fact of the matter is this, these people have probably way more to offer than the negative nancy talking shit. Because these people made something out of themselves. They went to great lengths to achieve that beauty. Especially the "gym-bros." Do you even know how many years of hard work and dedication are necessary to get such a body? These men are not stupid. Quite the opposite. And as someone who has the best ideas when at the gym, because the movement of the body increases the blood flow to your brain, I can tell you. A healthy body makes you a better person. There I said it, if you're fat and weak, your opinion doesn't count, and you're less of a person. Harsh? Yes, but the truth. You are less than what you could be, aren't you? You know exactly what your body could be if you put in the work. But you don't, so you are less. Simple logic. Become more than you are now. Maximize yourself. Maximize your physicality.

BEAUTY IS POWER

Nature in its purest form is beautiful,
breathtaking. Beauty would not be so heavily
emphasized by nature itself if it wouldn't inherit
a certain amount of power. Mankind chooses
the most beautiful things. In any situation.

People don't like to hear that, but beautiful people have it easier on average. And the reason would be obvious. Let's call them "not-so-lucky-on-looks-people" hate you for saying that, but they actually support the power of beauty every day themselves. How? Do you buy the ugliest car you can find? Or the best looking you can afford? Are the best looking ones the most expensive ones or the ugly ones? (Few exceptions, I know). Do you pick the most beautiful flower from a field, or a rotten, ugly one? Do you buy the best-looking clothes for you, or ratched, old, ruined shirts? (Unless you can't afford better). We choose beauty every day in everything we do. We also know that nicely prepared food actually tastes better, despite being the exact same food. Our brain reacts differently to it. Yet, people come in and say, you shouldn't choose your partner on looks. You shouldn't choose him/her solely on looks, yes. But it is a vital point. Everyone disagreeing with this is lying to themselves. Desire cannot be negotiated, and neither can attraction. If you aren't attracted to someone physically, you will have a hard time (or soft time) when you're up for sex.

It is through this twisted way of shaming people for being shallow that ugly people, or rather, people not putting effort in their appearance, try to create a power surge from beauty. Beauty is power, and there is nothing you can do about it. You can shame people for looking for beauty, but the nature of things will never change. I strayed away from that for too long. I bought the lies of society, that looking for beauty is bad. But, deep down, it always felt wrong to not do that. Once I actively fixed myself, and started to enjoy my own beauty, crafted in the gym and the kitchen, I started to appreciate beauty in nature again. The symmetry of things, their meaning, and the pleasure of looking at nice things are not to be ignored. We always worshipped beauty, and we still should keep that up. Mostly, because we will do it anyway, even if we force ourselves not to enjoy it.

And this is where beauty is power. It doesn't matter how hard you try to suppress it, beauty will always win. Through the products you buy, or the mating partner you choose. If you are beautiful, your chances are higher to succeed. This won't ever change. Because it hasn't ever changed. In thousands of years. Beautiful people get offered better opportunities in business or career. Beautiful people have access to a variety of more partners, and beautiful people are just healthier. Because, apart from the genetic lottery, there is a lot you can do to increase your beauty value. Eat properly, exercise, don't smoke, don't booze drink, don't masturbate. All of this is true for men and women. If you preserve your youthful beauty as long as possible, you will have better chances in life. I am not a fan of plastic surgery, because it rarely looks natural, maybe except for well-done boob jobs, but other than that, it is somehow noticeable. However, you can correct your teeth, you can get a proper haircut, grooming, proper clothes that fit you, the lot. All of this will increase your beauty, and thus your power.

This ugly society canceled beauty, and therefore it is trying to drag you down to their shitty level of ugliness. Look at cities as I mentioned at the beginning of this chapter. Where do you rather live? Look at the male and female beauty, who do you rather want to be with? Stop believing their lies that the appearance doesn't matter. It does. Very much so. And if you're neurotic about your appearance, stop being a weak cunt. Get the work in and make the best out of it. You won't bend nature to your will, but you can be closest to it and reap the rewards.

PART VIII
ANTI-SOCIAL MEDIA

The world you display and the world you live in should be as similar as possible. If they aren't, you are living a lie. And living a lie will steal your happiness. Live in reality, enjoy reality.

Social Media really has nothing to do with socializing. Not just because socializing needs a real person or more in front of you, because you need to work with mimics, gestures, energies, etc, but also because socializing is something positive. We need it as humans. It makes us feel better to interact with other humans. However, Social Media as we know it is Anti-Social Media. It is 99% negative, projection, hate, death threats, and shit-talking other people. And that's just Tweeter. If you go on Instagram, you have a Sims-Style display of a life no one lives which has nothing to do with socializing either.

And the reason for this is emotions. Heavy emotions are driving us to share stuff. If something really bad happens, that's what you tell your friends. Which is exactly the model of these big platforms. The most shared news are always very negative, outraging, or triggering. Now, about 3.5 billion people use social media every day. For hours. It's always funny to me when people install that app which shows you how many hours you looked at your phone that day. The lack of awareness is really a pandemic in this world. That said, these hours you spend on social media each day are usually filled with negativity from bad news around the world, outraging stories of genderfluid people and all that, or images from your friends' lives which are seemingly so much better than yours. What do you gain from that? Exactly. You hate your life. Not only is the whole world fucked, but all your friends also have it better, and your life sucks.

That being said, you need to realize something. Everyone is just winging life. Nobody has it all figured out. It might seem like it, but your friends posting those heavily filtered images on Instagram pay a heavy debt for their Mercedes, or their house. Anyone who owns a house knows this. They only share the best moments, never the worst, which they ultimately have. Now, granted, when you hang out with your married couple of choice, you never know if their sex-life is healthy, or if they fight constantly, beat their kids/wife, etc. People are very good at hiding their flaws. But you can sometimes see through the bullshit. And this is a skill you need to learn and train. When someone, for example, makes jokes about their sex-life, this usually indicates they are unsatisfied with it and try to subtly communicate to their partner that they should do something. This is usually done by the woman, but weak men do the same these days. This is just one example. If someone is bragging with their new Mercedes, but they can only afford the cheapest pizza when you're out eating, you know what's up. But you can't see that truth on social media. You need to be around people to know what they are really like.

And this is important if you want to know who to follow, and who to get your info from on social media. My corner of Twitter for example (the self-help gurus) have a ton of people who literally are con-artists. They say all these things of hustling constantly, fighting yourself, and all that, sell you a nice course on how to do it, and then they watch three hours of Netflix. That's why social proof is so important. It is literally a substitution for being around real people where you could realize if they're LARPing or not.

However, for your average Joe, this isn't important, they don't want to improve themselves anyway because it's work. And who wants to work when they just came home from work where they scrolled social media for hours? See, social media is really bad for you in most cases. Facebook, Instagram, and all that have algorithms to show you the most outrageous shit. Twitter is pretty much the only platform that can be positive because what you see is dependent on who you follow. So you design your feed yourself. This also creates an echo chamber of some sort, but at least it isn't fully negative all the time. Which is why I am mostly on Twitter. And even I, although I make money from it, am too much on it. For a reason.

DOPAMINE

He who knows how to stop himself from
engaging in easy pleasures rises above the
average within mere seconds.

When you unlock your phone and check Twitter or any other platform, you do this because of an addiction. People don't like to be told they are addicted to something, but again, if something changes your behavior, you are addicted. I am for sure. Sometimes, when I am doing something, I feel that urge to switch tabs to Twitter and see the new notifications and likes on my Tweets. This is the dopamine working. It's the pleasure chemical in your body. And if you like something, you want more of it.

So you see these people mindlessly scrolling their Facebook feed, although there really isn't anything new on there. Watch these people closely and you see very well their impression on their faces. They aren't happy. Because there is only negativity or lame jokes on Facebook. But they still have the urge to scroll it, because maybe someone likes their post, or they find something they can share (online or with you) to gain social clout. And through this dopamine release, these companies managed to make billions of mindless drones, trenched in negativity, sharing their message.

Social Media is a worldwide, billions-of-people-scaled test of people's mentality. Something, mankind has never managed to do so far. And slowly, but surely, we realize how bad it is for our health. A lot of people (me included) recommend dopamine fasting. It's like porn. You get desensitized to it. Too much of anything makes you numb to it. That's why these jokes you see there aren't funny anymore, but they might've been funny if a friend told it. That's why you can't get it up after you watched too much porn, you're desensitized to sexuality or the female body. You also get desensitized to negative news. You see them every day, so it's nothing special if someone shot up a school. "Well, it's somewhat common now." Really? A person being so isolated and fucked up, that they use a rifle to kill a bunch of kids is common? What a great society!

On top of that, social media is abused to influence elections, spread narratives, and change society. It is much more than just talking to people and sharing news. But none of it, we really need. Do we? Wouldn't it be much better to really talk to people instead of commenting under their tweets? And I say this as someone whose journey to conquering themselves was triggered (not only, but also) through a Twitter thread I randomly came by. It has positives, but they are very rare compared to the negatives.

INSTAPORN

Nothing in this world is for free. Sometimes the cost is just very well hidden.

Instagram is for women what porn is for men. In the female beauty chapter I went over this topic a little bit, but let's dive deeper because it is important. You see all these Instagram girls posting semi-nude pics of themselves, with tons of makeup, and filtered to hell. And they get unlimited attention from thirsty dudes. And this has another issue for men. Because, as I said (multiple times now), women want a man's attention. That is what you can steer your relationship with. If she doesn't behave properly, is being annoying, and nagging you, you could just remove attention, which would make her rethink her decisions. That said, with millions of dudes readily sending male attention her way, she really doesn't need it. Of course, real attention from you is still different than Instagram attention, but you can't deny that there is a similarity, and it makes it easier for women to get their fix. It's virtually the same as porn is for men and the women have an issue with it. Why do you think, women are so mad about a man watching porn? Because she knows quite well, sex is her tool to get you to do what she wants. Any woman knows, consciously or not, that with her sexuality she can influence your decisions to a certain degree. If you're a weakling, then even more so. But if you get sex at any second of your day, readily available, with the hottest ladies, in any position, she loses power. Just like you're mad, even though you might not understand why, when she talks to other men, or hangs around on Instagram, chatting other dudes, and sending them heart-emojis. She is gaining the male attention somewhere else when she should only get it from you. Just like you get sex from somewhere else, when you should only get it from her. You don't even need to open

Pornhub. Instagram works for men as well. You just need to find one of the millions of accounts on IG where beautiful women wear nothing but lingerie in sexual poses. That is already sexualized enough for you to get your fix. So in the end, we created two methods for both sexes to lose power in their relationship. Well done, society!

With this in place, I wish I would be surprised about the state of marriage and long-term relationships. People hate when you say it, but relationships, sometimes, are a power-struggle. It is, what it is. But when you remove both parties' possibilities to exert their power to have their needs met, well, what are you left with? Two people hanging around, which could jump ship at any moment because there is nothing to lose. And that is what Instagram has created. An escape for both sexes of their responsibilities towards their partner. Think about the basis of marriage. You decide to be with that one person forever, no one else involved. It's a commitment. But it also gives you a certain frame around your relationship. If there are problems, you need to fix them. That is why marriage is a vow in front of family and friends. It's not lightly done, you commit. But now, when sex or attention don't work out, you can just go somewhere else to get it, instead of fixing the problem itself! And unfixed issues will eventually haunt you. The price for mistakes always has to be paid. Sooner or later. And since we delay it so heavily, it usually ends up in divorce. People call me crazy for reading so much into an app to share pictures of your food, but it's really not that simple. And, well, thinking it's really not much more than food pics is a sign of what our current culture and society are about: Not thinking deeply enough about issues. Just seeing the surface and making it shinier with a nice filter.

PART IX
GODS

A society without gods is doomed to fail. Mankind needs an overseer to keep his chaotic nature in balance. If you don't have godly rules to follow, you will end up in Chaos itself. God is who creates order.

Let me preface this chapter real quick. This is not designed to make you believe in any deity. I couldn't care less to be honest. My point is, that I think, current society would be much better off if we didn't decide to kill god.

See, Nietzsche called the death of god. And we killed him. God, not the German. I always thought he meant this literally and I was confused by it. Especially since Nietzsche was an atheist. But he meant it metaphorically. He meant Christianity and all its inherent morality. And that's where I wholeheartedly agree. I have talked about morals before, but this chapter goes a bit deeper. For decades now, we made fun of people believing in any god. We laughed at them for being so "caged-into" their beliefs. Enlightenment brought us space! We could see the world without being tucked in by a god who gives nothing but rules, right? Well, wrong. Just look at what it brought us. The sexual revolution, which I already said, was more a drawback than anything else. Spoiled brats as kids who will never achieve anything worth noting and are a general pain in the ass in everyday situations. Weak fathers who can't fight for shit, and thus, could never protect their family. As well as being mentally weak, which explains the spoiled brats. And nagging, insufferable cunts as wives, which lost any sense for femininity and bring nothing to the table but their bodies and reproductive organs.

Cynical? Hell, yes! But important to wake you up to reality and remove your love goggles for this "free" society which isn't free at all. We gave up all rules that had been implemented by Christianity for the slavery of our limbic system. The reason these rules were made, was to stabilize society. I am sorry to break it to you, rebellious leftists, but anarchy is not a desirable state of society. People see anarchy for being without government. But the word actually means "a state of disorder." Chaos. Pure, unbridled chaos. As opposed to order, which makes for a healthy society. All anarchy does, is make it impossible to leave your house, because you might be robbed at any point. Without the robber being prosecuted. That said, don't mix up the Church with the state. Jordan Peterson once divided this quite well. The state makes legal rules. Rules you have to follow. The Church makes meta rules. Rules you should follow, to keep life in order. And here is where people always get confused because they don't understand me. I don't believe in God, but I believe in Religion.

See, personally, I don't think there is any form of higher deity sitting in the skies, judging people, and deciding if you go to hell and drink with Lucifer or if you go to the Silver City. But I do see why man invented god. He is the kind of father figure (hence why he is male, you screeching feminists), because he sits above it all, rules, and judges. And while he is a good god, he also has a capacity for evil. Which is necessary, if you want to keep your sheep in place. He is like a shepherd. He guides where to go, what path to take. But the sheep might run around weirdly, if not contained. So he has his shepherd dogs (the rules, enforced by pastors and so on) to tell the sheep where to go. He doesn't interact directly with the sheep, but he is the one who guides them. That is the slight difference to the family father. He still interacts directly with his sheep, but the rules are his, and they are to be enforced if he wants a stable family. Think about it, if you have no rules in your family at home, everyone can do whatever they want, how do you think this will go down? Yes, Chaos. Again. And that's where I believe in Religion, but not god. I think the Bible is a conglomeration of the best life lessons we got from our ancestors. Packed in a story, with an overseeing god to use a little bit of fear, so the sheep actually do as they're told. If you read the Bible as a non-fiction book, literally, without god being a huge deity, just as a guideline book, then it is basically a self-improvement book to get your life in order. And that's where I believe in. You can still believe in God, I don't care, but you have to realize that these rules were made to keep masses of humans living and working together.

Obviously, all of the religions were designed a long time ago. So some rules are pretty outdated. I am not saying you should stone people that don't believe. I mean, common sense should dictate that, but I am aware there is a certain lack of that trait these days. However, we should make a new new testament. The guidelines to keep society in check adapted with some newfound knowledge. That said, there is an important footnote. The newfound knowledge needs to come from a place of experience and tested knowledge. Not ideology. Because I know, leftists would immediately jump it, and call for equality of the genders. Get lost. We lived in our natural states of both genders for millions of years and it worked fine. Since you decided to bring in equality of outcome, marriages went down the drain, both genders lost their nature, and cuckoldry is suddenly a thing. Basically, anarchy lite. So to stop that from happening in both ways, current society would benefit greatly from Religion. However, it is "enforced" doesn't matter. Via a god, or through law. But rules are what make people behave properly. Of course, this also means giving up freedom, but you know that discipline equals freedom, as I mentioned in the "Forced Freedom" chapter. Rules, and fear of the implications of breaking them, keeps humans from giving in to their vices, their limbic system, and gives them the opportunity to become something greater than just monkey who learned how to drive a car. We can be so much more than just numbed down NPCs. We can be the heroes in our story. But for that, we need to follow rules. Any hero ever had rules he followed. Religiously (get it?). Because they gave him the possibility to be more than just human. Transcend time, write history, and change the world. If you always give in to your animalistic desires, you change nothing. You just exist on this planet. Like an animal. Whereas if you follow rules, you can become a god. And change society for good.

THE EVIL CHRISTIAN GOD

*Punishment is necessary. Without
punishment, rules are worthless. It is the
respect of the consequences of your actions that
makes you decide not to indulge in self-
destroying behavior.*

The Christian god (too bad he doesn't have a cool name) was a notorious serial killer. While he did create mankind and thus gave us our existence on this planet, he also is known throughout the Bible to really get mad sometimes. And I am not talking about the 10 plagues he sent to the Egyptians for enslaving the Israelites. Or killing all humans, except Noah. Maybe you're familiar with the story of him having 20-something kids mauled by a bear because they made fun of a man being bald. Now, obviously, we need to see that these stories were written by men. But why would they write the creator of mankind so negatively sometimes? So evil, and ungiving? Well, because punishment is necessary.

You see, these days we tell parents to not discipline their children because it breaks their spirit or some shit like that. Which is weird, because we have disciplined our children physically for thousands, probably millions of years, and we came out just fine. Look what we managed to create. Yet, for some reason, all of a sudden it is bad and makes for bad people. However, when you look at how people, especially children, and young people, behave these days, compared to history, I think the evidence that this is backward is quite clear. The problem is the father of the family, the god in this little universe is not punishing bad behavior. And this starts way before kids are even in place. Man these days are so weak, they are afraid to punish their wife if they misbehave. And I am not talking about domestic violence. I am talking about removing attention or leaving, not giving her what she unrightfully demands. Women are a lot like children in that regard, and I always said, a woman is great training for having kids. She will test all your boundaries, and if you don't set them, she will absolutely take everything from you. And she will resent you for it.

Look, boundaries, enforced boundaries, and rules are important, because it tells that you have rules for yourself. And you can be respected for it. If you have no rules, or you don't enforce them, nobody would respect you. They can do whatever they like, you put up with it. This is why men are so confused when they "do everything to please their wife" and they still end up cheating with Chad. See, that isn't solely some evil hypergamous hivemind thingy from her. It's because you cannot be respected! By showing her that you have no rules, boundaries, and limits, she thinks she can get away with it. And a lot of the times, she actually can. It's the same with your kids. If you never discipline them, they think they can get away with stealing, smoking, whoring around, even though you tell them differently. Words are meaningless, actions need to follow suit.

And this is why our Christian god sometimes went apeshit. To show mankind who is boss. After all, he created us (like you created the life of your kids). This isn't a display of power for his own ego. It is to tell his creation that there are consequences to all actions. A truth a lot of people tend to forget these days. Obviously, God had to use larger scale punishment for the whole of mankind for all of them to notice. You don't need to send 10 plagues to all women to tell them that promiscuity is not desirable. You do it by just not giving them attention. So stop paying random average women money for not even stripping down on their OnlyFans accounts. Anyway, the point is, punishment has been canceled in our culture, and it shows. Look at what people are like, especially in "progressive" big cities. There are literally no rules, and if they are, they aren't enforced. Young men are doing nothing but getting boozed up each weekend, porn, videogames. Young women are fucking every dick they find, and couldn't even be bothered to care about birth control, and thus aborting a ton of kids. Or they sell their bodies online to weak losers who masturbate to them in their basement. Kids misbehave constantly, hitting strangers, knocking stuff over, yelling, screaming in public places. I can keep this list going. Decency is the first thing that died when we stopped enforcing behavior rules. Compare it to back in the day, when kids were grounded or got a light spanking when they misbehaved. Meeting strangers was a pleasure. You could talk to them, talk to their kids, etc. Try talking to a random family at a supermarket these days. They will look at you weirdly, while their kid is probably humping your leg.

Rules are what discerns us from animals. They only follow their animalistic desires (hence the name, duh). They don't have a consciousness as we do. They don't set advanced rules in their tribes. Or at least, they rarely do. So, since we stopped punishing bad behavior, we actually reverted the progress we made in evolution and turned back to be more like animals. Which is funny, because feminists will tell you, that punishing women and children for their bullshit is being animalistic. It is quite the opposite, but feminists always have it backward.

Anyway, men were punished as well, don't get me wrong here. Back in the day, if you didn't achieve anything worthwhile by at least 30 years of age, you were an outcast. You were a disgrace to your family, tribe, and society. These days, men grow physically but revert mentally. All I see are a ton of manchildren. And these manchildren have other children. What do you expect them to become? Decent humans? How's that going to work? And when they end up punishing their kids or wife, finally, they lash out and go too far. They build up so much resentment over time, that when they finally let it go, they virtually explode in pure rage. That's domestic violence for you. It is always weak men who do that. You might think a strong man can be dangerous. You have no idea what a mentally weak man is capable of. Trust me, I know, because I have been that guy in the past. I didn't hit my wife or anything. But I felt the resentment building up, and the thoughts I had were not pleasant. Thank god I never acted on it. Some men do. These days, nothing phases me, really. I set clear rules, and if they are broken, there is one warning, and then there is punishment.

Why am I so chill about shit getting thrown at me? Because I punish myself. No, not cutting wrists. I don't let myself be embraced by animalistic pleasures all the time. I set rules for myself. And if I break them, I will be punished. This behavior sets me up for a strong mind. Because I know I have myself under control. Most people in this society never do that. They indulge in every easy pleasure they find because there is no punishment. No external punishment. And internal, they don't even think about it. Because the short-term pleasure feels nice, right? But what about long-term?

Remember, as a man, you are the Godfather in that family. You lead, you set the tone, and you decide where the family goes. If you don't, you will have Chaos. From time to time, if your peers don't behave, you need to punish them for their own good. Of course, they won't like it, but you know they need it and it is best for them. It is in their interest, and deep down they know it. It's just at that moment, they don't realize. This is also why women and children will love you even more if you have strong boundaries. They know they can rely on you because you display that you lead yourself, and thus are a strong leader to follow.

APOLLO

Puny man needs an image to strive for. An idol, a god. Said god is an image that can never be achieved by the mortal. This is the basis of human evolution and success. To strive for the impossible.

Apollo or Apollon is one of the most complex gods in greek history. He was the god of light, poetry, archery, music, dance, truth, prophecy, healing, and many more things. All of which is overall positive, which is exactly what he is. The basis of humanity. He is supposed to be the lighting symbol of what a human should be. A positive force in this world, changing it through truth and poetry, enjoying it through music and dance, healing through being great. He gave people an image of what to be. A god is always an idol, and an idol always judges you. You strive to be that person or deity in your own life, because it is the idol you want to be. This is again why I talk about these gods so much. As I said, I don't believe in deities. The Greek gods were invented to keep society in place. By giving them rules, morals, and idols to strive for.

We never really ditched gods altogether, they just changed. From deities sitting on the Olymp to a man sitting in the sky, to the man sitting at the CEO Desk of Amazon. Or wearing a shirt with a number and his name on the back. We also search for idols to strive for. People better than us, people we want to mimic and implicate their lifestyle. That is fine and well, the problem is, that we changed from Gods like Apollo, which were intentionally designed to be unachievable (thus gods) to actual, real-life people with all their flaws.

See, if you have in idol which can never be achieved, you have something to strive for all your life. You can never be a god like Apollo. But when the media is reporting from the most famous golf player that he cheated on his wife, that makes him human. You can relate to him. And consciously or not, this also makes you drop some of your efforts. Because you realize, your idol has flaws, so you manifesting flaws isn't that bad. You can still be your idol, despite your flaws. And this is the fallacy of not having unreachable idols and literal gods. We stopped striving for the best. We settle for the mediocre. Which is heavily reflected in the state of society. Both genders which are only a shell of what they could be, and families, which are split, and hate each other, except on Facebook.

And this is where I come back to the fact that we should have Religion. Through those Gods and idols, we get a sense of our potential. What we could be if we followed their rules, their guidelines, and lifestyles. People say the devil is sneaky, and works in ways where you don't realize what's happening. But I think he was very overt when he literally killed all our images and our worshipping of the gods. This society is run by the devil. Chaos, envy, hate, evil, and cheap pleasure rule the world these days. All of Lucifer's tools. A lot of people do live in a literal hell, but a lot of you guys don't even realize that the ground underneath you is burning all day. Your soul is slowly being sucked out of your body through the pain you have to go through each day. But you can fix it yourself. The devil only has power if you give it to him. If you give in to your vices, your easy pleasures, and animalistic instincts. Start worshipping the real gods, start following some religious rules, and see yourself turn into Apollo. The idol, the god, the best version of yourself.

HELIOS

Man has operated under the sun for millions of years. To neglect Helios and his unending powers, is to neglect an immense source of energy. Do so at your own peril.

Helios was the god of the sun or the sun itself in the form of a god in ancient Greek mythology. He was considered a somewhat minor god, because, well, the sun was abundant in ancient Greece. They had strong summers and very mild winters. Sunny days pretty much all year round, so Helios was not that important to worship. He was around all the time. However, the ancient greeks very heavily relied on the sun. They build solariums in their homes, which basically where rooms without a roof where the sun would shine through. Hippocrates prescribed sunbathes to ill people to heal better. All sorts of diseases were healed with the sun. And it did work. The Greeks also exercised and trained in open-air gyms. In contrast to us these days, training in dark, badly lit or filled with artificial light gyms. And as you saw in the picture from the male beauty chapter, those men had great bodies. They didn't use any supplements, steroids or all that, because it didn't exist. What they used, was the sun. They trained almost every day, under the sun, for hours. There are multiple topics why I bring this up, and why you should start worshipping Helios by selling your house, moving to a sunny state, and buying a tent to live outside.

I'm kidding, but firstly, the sun is a very vital part of human being. We lived under it for millions of years. In other words, we evolved to use it, because it is a great source of energy. Only in recent decades, we decided to live more inside than outside. We know now for a fact, due to multiple studies and research, that you need daily exposure to the sun. It produces vitamin D which is important for your organs, cognitive ability, and vital functions. We also know, it makes you happier (Helios is known to be the god "who gives joy to mortals"), but most importantly, it helps growing muscle, reducing fat, and producing testosterone! All of which are related to each other and multiplied by being exposed to the sun. You actually produce the most testosterone when you put your balls in sunlight. I am dead serious about this. That said, I wouldn't want to advocate to you guys to go out there having them hang out in the sun. I mean, if that's your thing, go ahead, but it might make for weird conversations.

Anyway, this fact should tell you how important the sun truly is to your bodily health. And as you learned already, the mind and body are heavily intertwined. So the intelligent reader will already have made the connection to our current society. When you sit inside all day, no sunlight whatsoever, staring at artificial light from a screen, and then you go home, sitting in front of another screen with even less sunlight, your body is not producing enough vitamin D. Plus all the other health benefits from being exposed to Helios.

186

Our lifestyle actively weakens you every day. But it gets worse.

Secondly, we try to get the sun out wherever we go. Even if we are in the sun. Sunglasses, I only learned recently are very bad for you. Apparently, it is crucial that sunlight gets into your system through the eyes. You don't need to stare directly into the sun, but you should be exposed to indirect sunlight (via reflection from surfaces) by being in the sun without sunglasses. However, this culture told us it is cool to have sunglasses. You look cool, and, well, you can look at cleavage without being burned. Just like looking into the sun. However, these things naturally steal you of a great source of energy and increasing health in your body. The majority of people are very unhealthy. And while a lot of it is due to bad diets and no movement whatsoever, a big part is also due to not being in the sun at all, and not being exposed to its energy.

The ancient Greeks probably were physically our human prime. They had insane fit bodies and set a lot of records that haven't been broken till today. Solely because they lived very differently, and properly used nature's abundant energy sources.

At this point, you might be asking yourself how they didn't get sunburnt when being in the sun all day. Well, sunburn is a new-age phenomenon. If you are never exposed to the sun, naturally, your skin can't handle it when you finally are exposed to it for hours. If you grow up in the sun all day, your skin is used to it. And if you keep it moisturized, which is what the ancient greeks did, there is no need for sunscreen, which those people didn't even have. Obviously. And now you might be wondering why we put that sunscreen with hundreds of chemicals onto our biggest organ (the skin...). Well, because our skin isn't used to the exposure. But you still could do it. By the only way that works and has always worked for everything. Slowly increasing adversity to make it resilient. As in, start slowly exposing yourself to the sun without sunscreen. You gradually build a tolerance to it. It's like that dude who injects snake venom into his body. He started with very low doses and increased it over time. He looks fucking fabulous. Anyway, for the Helios exposure, use olive oil, or some fatty, natural moisturizers for your skin to stop it from drying out. Increase the exposure slowly, and you will never need to put a chemical-loaden cream on your body. Obviously, society doesn't want you to know that, because sunscreen is a billion-dollar market. Imagine the people would learn that you don't need that at all. Huge market just gone!

Anyway, Helios is your new god. Worship him! Get out of there and take his energy he gives so freely. The benefits you will notice are so insane, you won't believe it. I stopped wearing sunglasses. Your eyes will get used to it quickly. At first, it will be too bright, don't worry, it'll get better. Your eyes need time to adapt because you never really used them. Just like your skin will need that time. Easiest way to do it is to incorporate one hour or even half an hour of walking at noon each day. After your midday meal, just go outside and walk a bit in the sun. And if you live in a country that rarely has sun, well, tough luck. Time to move.

HADES

Memento mori.

Hades is the god of death and the lord of the underworld. And for some reason, he is always pictured very dark and evil. Well, maybe the reason is that people are literally afraid of death. But why is that? Maybe this chapter alone explains a few prior chapters. We are so afraid of death these days, especially in the west (other societies celebrate death for example) that we try to avoid it as much as possible. Even for other people like the mentally ill, even though it might be a relief for them. But it's not just our own decay. The death of your pets, a friends' pet, or death of animals in general, so we end up not eating them. Although meat is one of the most nutritious foods for us.

All of it is rooted in fear. The fear of the unknown. It is this fear of not knowing what will happen when we die, that keeps us afraid of it. We are always only afraid if the outcome is unknown. If you ride into battle, well knowing that you will die, you don't fear anything. The outcome is clear. However, soldiers didn't always know they would die or not in their fights back in the day. But they still decided to go in. Not only because they decided to be brave. Because bravery is a decision, not a trait. But also because they weren't afraid of death as we are today. And a big reason for this is how we live.

Our lives are one big debt until we retire. We work jobs we hate for the majority of our lives until we finally quit it at 70 years old. This is when we finally can start living. At least, that's what we've been sold for decades. Do your duty to work most of your healthy lifespan to pay off the debt towards society you were born with until you can finally relax later. For the ancient soldier, there was no retirement waiting. Succeeding his training as a soldier and finally fighting for his people was the pinnacle of his life. If he died at this moment, there wasn't much lost. His work was already his life. He wasn't looking forward to something late in his life, which he never knows if it will ever come.

And this is why we are afraid of dying early. Because we haven't lived at all. We only worked. Vacation once a year is not living, it is a short escape of your every day, pretty grim life. Small meals on the way to the great banquet at 70 years old. You've been drip-fed these short spans of "life" for years before you actually get to really enjoy this wonderful existence. Now, obviously, I am not saying that every person in the past always had it better. Slavery, being born a low-class citizen and all that. They didn't even have that retirement to look forward to. My point is, the image society paints you each day is a lie. It is evil and crooked. When you are finally 70 years old and spent your best years on meaningless and irrelevant jobs, you won't have enough energy to finally enjoy life. Mostly because you've been eating shit all your life and neglecting your health.

And so we project our own dismay onto any other living being. Our pets absolutely need to spend the maximum of their lifetime, before they are allowed to die. No matter what great moments you already had with your dog, he needs to live as long as possible. Solely because you are afraid of your own emotions and grief. And because he shall have lived the best life, as long as possible. Because this is how you see your own life, and naturally any other living being lives the same, right?

Eating animals is cruel! They deserve to live a free life, on a wide, green field, enjoying their very being. Again, because you are afraid to kill another living being for your own needs. And not because you're so empathetic, it is to make you feel better that you saved another life from not living the shit life you have. It is hypocritical and weak. Humans have eaten animals for our entire life span. Animals kill each other all the time. It is the basis of nature. You are neglecting your own nature, out of spite towards your own life. Now, obviously, we as humans, due to our unending greed have done some evil things to animals on this planet. When a lion kills a hyena, he does it to survive. It has a need. We have tortured them, ruined their environment for a consumerist mall, and the way we produce meat én masse these days is really very unethical. Yes, there are issues with this. Definitely. I am not denying this. But remember why you are not wanting to eat animals. The real reason for it. Be honest with yourself. You are projection the misery of your own life onto other animals. The chicken in the factory didn't live a great life. But the chicken on a farm, who had some fun so far with the other chickens, and now dies a greater cause to help a human survive another day, do you really think this is so bad for said chicken?

Your ego is really what is afraid of death. If you are at peace with yourself, accepted that we all die at some point anyway, and this is the way of things, then what are you afraid of? We all can die at any given moment. People's hearts have suddenly stopped beating. You can be run over the next step you take on the street. You can be robbed, shot at, whatever. Any given moment you could be dead. And deep down, you know that. So you live all your life, afraid of every step you take to prolong death until after you finally started living late in your existence. Instead, try living now. And no, this doesn't mean "yolo" and quit your job, screw everything, and just indulge in pleasures. Whatever you want to be, want to do, aim to do it now, or soon. If you want to travel the world for years, then build something that provides enough money to do so. You only do have this one life, that is what "yolo" or its original "Carpe diem" really means. Enjoy the day, you could be dead tomorrow. This doesn't need to be huge consumerist dreams you've been sold. It may just mean to hug your wife today, give her a kiss, and enjoy the love you two share. It might mean, playing with your child in the sandbox. It might mean, having a beer with your friends. It might mean, writing this book, because you truly want to give something to the world.

Memento mori. Remember death. It lures on each corner of life. And Hades comes when he decides to, not when you decided you "lived" enough at 80. Live now, make the best of each day, and celebrate death for what it is: it gives meaning to your life. Without death, your life would be a repetition of the same old things. Just like a good book series or movie series needs to end at some point, so life needs to end, to give it a frame before it gets repetitive and boring.

NOTHINGNESS

The universe is so vast and big, it mostly
consists of nothing. Emptiness. We are but a
small speck in this vastness. In the grand
scheme of things, our existence is irrelevant.
Remembering this each day, paradoxically will
give your life meaning.

If you haven't read Carl Sagan's book "Pale blue dot" you absolutely need to. It will humble your existence on this planet. Mostly because of this picture right here:

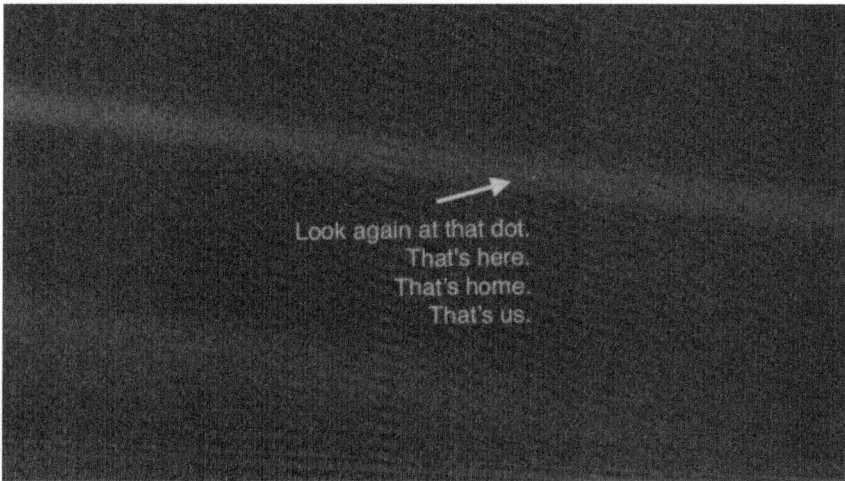

Look again at that dot.
That's here.
That's home.
That's us.

This is the Earth. Photographed from the Voyager spacecraft 3.7 billion miles away. Now, stop reading quickly over these lines here for a second. Slow down. Breathe. And think about this image. Look at it, take it in. Everything that has ever happened to us. Every king, every emperor, every man, every woman, every father, mother, child, sister, brother; every killer, every saint, every president, every homeless person, every loved one, every partner and love of one's life has lived on this small fleck in the vastness of the universe. Our whole range of emotions, possibilities, and everything mankind has ever done happened on this spot. Around us? Nothing. Cold, hard, nothing.

Think about yourself right now. Wherever you are reading this book. You are sitting somewhere on this planet, while stationary in your place, still moving with 67,000 miles per hour around Helios in the vastness of nothingness. Everything you ever did, everything you will ever do doesn't really matter in the grand scheme of the universe. And this is exactly why it matters. See, we constantly search for meaning in this life. We want to ask our creator, the universe itself, or Jordan Peterson what the meaning of life truly is. Why are we on this planet? Why is this planet in this universe? Why do we exist? What is the point? We live, we die, repeat. But why? This question bothers a lot of people, and it did bother me. It might even drive you insane if you really think about it. But the answer to this is actually pretty simple. You answer it with a question: Does it really matter?

Imagine there was a god you could actually ask why we are here. The answer would be disappointing no matter what it is. Why? Because your search would finally be over. It's like at the end of a TV show you followed for years. The end of the last season, when everything is revealed. It's almost always disappointing. And even if they stuck the landing, and end with a glorious bang, you are still left over with nothingness. That void in you, because something has been taken out of your life. And you quickly search for a fix. An alternative for your chase. The meaning of life is the same. The question is what drives us. That is, what gives life meaning. The question if there is any meaning. It is like a TV show that never stops. We keep introducing new characters, killing off old ones, new catastrophes happen, constantly making and living new stories. And that is the meaning of life, keeping it up. Keep living.

Experiencing this very precious life we have, and making the best of it.

So, remembering each day, that nothing really matters, your preferred pronouns, your misogyny, your sexism, the size of your member, or how many followers you have on Twitter. None of it is important in any way. We occupy our time with this irrelevant stuff, instead of trying to maximize ourselves, and make the best out of this one life we have. You will die either way. We all do. And that's why we need to give the short blip of time we exist as living beings in this universe the most meaning we can do. By simply living it. By maximizing our human potential. Striving for things which seem impossible, until we do the impossible for the thousandth time. Killing ourselves in wars for millennia, saving each other from natural catastrophes for the thousandth time. Why? Because we're humans. We are flawed, as is everything in this life. And this is what gives our life meaning. The fact that we die at some point. And then we're probably reborn and do everything again. Or not. Who knows. All we know is this: put as much life into your life as possible. Try to leave a legacy, a culture, so future generations know of your struggles and can better mankind for good. Make us humans better. Everyone living right now is on the path to make mistakes, future generations can learn from. So we can make full use of this consciousness we have, but we don't really understand. Maybe, at some point we will accidentally come across an answer because we expanded our mind so far, the answer is obvious. I hope we never do because the chase for the answer is what keeps us going.

selfconquering.com

Because it's the only thing that counts. Maximizing your potential on this planet. In this universe of vast nothingness you create meaning by living to be the best you can be.

Email: alex@selfconquering.com
Twitter: https://twitter.com/selfconquering

If you want more from my triggering writing, sign up on my free newsletter and be informed, and maybe also get some discounts: https://selfconquering.com/signup

EPILOGUE

You made it this far. Congratulations. At this point, you're either raging and screaming about my misogyny and sexism, or I made a new friend. Nobody is going to read this and be like "Meh." So either way, I hope I opened your eyes and mind to a lot of truths about this society and our CANCEL CULTURE. But most importantly, I hope it helped to see how you can cope with this and still live a happy and successful life, despite the fact society is literally out there to stop you from achieving that.

I highly recommend you re-read a few chapters, especially the ones about your manhood. They are very important if you want to become a force to be reckoned with. and feel free to hand this book to your friends. It may help them, even though they will first be heavily raging about it.

If you find your mission as a man, if you lead, and if you have your physicality in check, you will ascend into new realms you didn't even know before. And there will be a certain calmness and strength to your behavior which might irritate you at first. I noticed this change quite strongly. I was confused at how calm I suddenly reacted in certain situations, how I almost didn't care sometimes, how I took charge and got shit done instead of talking about it. If you notice something similar, let me know!

But beware, changing yourself to become a real man, and behaving like that will trigger people around you. You will be called sexist, an asshole, and whatnot. This is just from people losing power over you. Naturally, they fight that. See it for what it is, you're gaining back control over your life, and therefore you will create enemies. Maybe even very close people. And depending on what your goals are, you might turn a whole group of people against you, which have been denying the truth for quite a while.

However, if you are at that point of your journey, your spirituality will be so high, it just doesn't matter at all. I have been called all sorts of things. If anything, it just gave me more confirmation that I am doing the right thing. As they say, life is like a videogame, you're on the right path when you meet enemies.

So go out there and become one with yourself. With your nature, your biology, your manhood. All of life's gifts are waiting for you when you put in the effort, time, and grit to go after them. Be the kind of man you want your daughter to marry. This is the mantra you need to follow. If you aren't that person, then you're not living life to your full potential. Bring back true masculinity by being an example. Lead by example. Show people how it's done, be brave, bold, direct, confident. Be leading, giving, forgiving, and dominant. Rebel against societies' questionable laws which so far, brought nothing but negativity and despair. Be a positive force in this life. While negative tweets work on Tweeter, reality is different. Positivity is what attracts people, life, and the universe. Be good, do good, and receive good.

MANkind is relying on you to be a man. You are a part of all men as a whole. Your part is to be what we should be. To be one of the shining lights of this sex to show what we're capable of. It is on every one of us. When you start your journey to greatness doesn't matter. It only matters that you start it.

I wish you all the best and feel free to contact me at any time.

And now go out there, and conquer yourself! So you can finally conquer this world.

Alexander
Reich

Printed in Great Britain
by Amazon

47158173R00119